PLEASANT PLACES

Short Essays on the Christian Life

By

Anthony F. Russo

Anthony F. Russo

PLEASANT PLACES

Short Essays on the Christian Life

ANTHONY F. RUSSO

Copyright © 2014 by Anthony F. Russo

Read more and sign up for the free newsletter at: www.anthonyfrusso.com.

Order additional copies and find out more at: www.pleasantplacesbooks.com.

Book reviews are important. Please consider leaving a book review at your favorite internet bookseller site. Thank you!

Cover photo is a view from the cliffs of Port Isaac, Cornwall, England © 2013 Anthony F. Russo.

Back cover photo by Allison Viscomi.

Photo of Felicia Bauerle: Family photo.

Unless otherwise indicated, all Scripture quotations are from The Holy Bible, English Standard Version® (ESV®), copyright © 2001 by Crossway, a publishing ministry of Good News Publishers. Used by permission. All rights reserved.

Pleasant Places

NIV is the New International Version. Holy Bible, New International Version®, NIV® Copyright © 1973, 1978, 1984, 2011 by Biblica, Inc.®

NKJV is the New King James Version. The Holy Bible, New King James Version Copyright © 1982 by Thomas Nelson, Inc.

KJV is the King James Version and is in the public domain.

A note about the capitalization of pronouns referring to God: I changed all the deity-related pronouns in the manuscript three times as I worked through this issue. Men I admire like R.C. Sproul, John MacArthur, and Paul Washer capitalize the pronouns. Randy Alcorn, the ESV Bible, and others do not. The latter do not do so out of disrespect but for consistency's sake. In the final days before publication I decided to leave pronouns relating to deity lowercase just to keep things simple.[1]

A note about citations: I have sought to properly cite all sources where possible. Where that was not possible I acknowledge that I heard the remark from somewhere.

Thank you to Amy and to Ed V. for helping me edit this book.

---

[1] See Randy Alcorn, "Why don't you capitalize 'he' when referring to God?"
http://www.epm.org/resources/2012/Apr/6/why-dont-you-capitalize-he-when-referring-god/

DEDICATION

To Jesus, the best second chance I ever had.

To Amy, the second-best second chance I ever had.

Pleasant Places

WHY I WROTE THIS BOOK

For a writer, a used book store is both a high and low. The high is seeing all the books and finding a good bargain on one or two (or ten). The low is seeing all those books and hearing that inner voice say the world has enough books already. For me that moment asks, "Why bother?"

Because.

Because in the end all we leave behind are our convictions. Whether we are a writer, an artist, a factory worker, architect, CEO or garbage man our core principles—be they vice or virtue—survive us. They are painted on canvas, spelled out on paper, towering into the sky as brick and steel and glass, or simply etched in the minds of those who know us best. A plumber who has the integrity to never do a shoddy job will leave his conviction in a thousand miles of properly installed pipes and fittings. Recently the maternity nurse who was there when my wife was born died. She left her convictions in a legacy of delivering, mending and caring. And parents, though I am not one, leave their convictions in the memories and values they instill in their children. We all have convictions and we all leave traces of them behind, like old books outlive their authors.

…Which brings me back to the used bookstore and why I wrote this book. Every author of every book on every shelf is either going to die or already has. Their convictions are left in their words. And I want my convictions to be left on a shelf for someone to discover some day. I want the world to know that Jesus Christ was God and came to earth, fully God and fully Man, over 2,000 years ago. He healed the sick, raised the dead and, though sinless, died on a cross as the only substitutionary payment for the sins of his own people. Three days later he rose from the dead, is seated with the Father in heaven, and will one day return to judge and to reign. And I want the world to know that this same Jesus raised *this* dead man to life in 2005.

I put these words out on my website on September 15, 2011:

> On this day in 2005 in a one-bedroom apartment in Tampa, Florida, by God's grace, I turned from the sinful life I was living and took God up on his tender, gracious offer to clean me up, forgive me for every sinful thing I ever said, thought, or did, and everything I ever would. Because Jesus died and rose again he offers new life. How could I not say yes to such a wonderful offer extended at such a cost to someone so undeserving of it?
>
> I am "into Jesus" because of his goodness and love, not out of any sense of trying to pay him back or cower under some kind of angry cosmic tyrant—infinitely far from it. If someone pulled you out of a burning car and saved your life and nursed you back to health you would want to tell everyone about that person so they could know him too—that's all I've been trying to do since that day. Thanks for reading this. I love you all very much and hope you might let me introduce to my Friend someday if you don't know him.

That is why I wrote this book. That is my conviction. And I pray by the end of this book it will be *your* conviction, and he will be *your* Friend too.

Pleasant Places

WHY YOU SHOULD READ THIS BOOK

In May of 2013 my wife and I took a trip to Cornwall, England. After two planes, one subway, one train, one taxi, and one adrenaline-pumping, mind-focusing first-time-driving-on-the-other-side-of-the-road experience, we made it to the small fishing village and tourist destination of Port Isaac. A short walk from our hotel was the view on the cover of the book you're holding. I was speechless at the beauty of the sights, sounds, and smells washing over and around us. Everything in that moment was perfect. I told Amy that if the Lord saw fit to take away my sight suddenly I would be thankful to have that beautiful view as the last thing I ever saw this side of heaven. That day on that Cornish cliff I thought to myself, *Every bit of effort that was required to get to this place was worth it.*

David, the writer of Psalm16 and so many of the psalms, had a similar experience. As he reflected on his life he declared that the Lord was his chosen portion, his cup, and the One who determined his lot. The "boundary lines" of his life, he wrote, had fallen to him in pleasant places. "Indeed," he said, "I have a beautiful inheritance." Whatever joys and hardships God worked in his life to bring him to such a beautiful panoramic survey of his life were, in his estimation, all worth it.

Living as a Christian brings with it "many dangers, toils, and snares" as John Newton wrote. Jesus promises his followers many wonderful things, but he also promises, "In the world you will have tribulation…" A disturbing thought, for sure. But he adds, "… take heart; I have overcome the world"

Anthony F. Russo

(John 16:33). Of all the pursuits and pastimes in this life, nothing compares to knowing Jesus Christ. Why should you read this book? Because the pleasant places God takes us, though sometimes difficult to arrive at, are entirely worth it.

Pleasant Places

TABLE OF CONTENTS

Dedication 4

Why I Wrote This Book 5

Why You Should Read This Book 7

Introduction 13

Did God Buy Your Lunch or Save You from Choking? 21

Everything Seemingly is Spinning Out of Control 25

If a Missionary Came to America 27

The Sword and the Handrail 30

He Walks Among the Lampstands 33

The Day I Learned I Could Do More 34

Lost and Found 36

Trouble Reading Through Leviticus? Know the Three C's 39

A Month of Blessings: Benefits of Being a Christian 42

Happy Birthday Miss Fleeda 45

He Breaks Our Chains in Pieces 47

He Really Will 49

What is it to Pray in Faith? 51

The Right Perspective Makes All the Difference 53

The Stamp Heard 'Round the World 55

Healed...to Serve 57

Staying Fixed on Jesus 58

Life in the Third Verse: It Is Well With My Soul 60

Faith Sets the Table 61

Led By Jesus: A Story of Reverent Imagination 63

God is Your Refuge 66

Two Places in this World 67

I Have Seen, I Know, I Have Come Down 69

The Choices We Make When No One is Watching 71

Christianity has Failed? 73

Favorite Examples of God's Mercy 75

Egypt After the Exodus 79

Jehovah Jireh: The Lord Provides 81

The Cloud, the Cross, and the Christ 82

Reflections on 1 Peter 1:1-5 84

What Does It Mean to Say "God is Sovereign"? 87

Cosmic Justice? Are You Sure You Want That? 89

Is it "Christian" to Feel Like You Have No Way Out? 91

Reflections on Work 94

The Curse is Gone, the Curse is Gone! Praise the Lord, the Curse is Gone! 96

That Defeated Tyrant, Death 98

The Four Criteria We All Use to Determine What We Believe 99

Spiritual Warfare 103

10 Reasons Church Matters 107

Pleasant Places

8 Essentials in a Good Church	110
The Futility of Man-Made Religion	116
No Less Days	118
What Does Your Facebook Profile Say About Your Faith?	122
How to Go to Heaven — In Five Words	126
In God's Bankruptcy Court	128
How Would You Introduce Yourself?	130
Suffering Weighed in the Scales	132
Creation in Six Literal, 24-Hour Days?	134
The Bible: Authority for Everything It Touches	135
We Can Trust the Bible, Part I	138
We Can Trust the Bible, Part II	141
More from Athanasius	144
But Can They Name Them?	146
In the Presence of the Great Dignitary	148
Peter's Evangelism Notes, Part I	150
Peter's Evangelism Notes, Part II	152
Prepare the Way, Everyday	154
Principles of Prayer	155
Worship Through Evangelism	159
"There is but a Step Between Me and Death"	160
Waiting	162

Do Not Be Deceived.. 169

A Dynasty of Grace 171

Trouble Praying?... 173

I Know a Secret 175

What Have You Done with the Bible? 177

A Walk Through A Cemetery 179

A Final Word: We're Almost Home.. 183

Pleasant Places

INTRODUCTION

The Lord is my chosen portion and my cup;
  you hold my lot.
The lines have fallen for me in pleasant places;
  indeed, I have a beautiful inheritance.
- Psalm 16:5,6

I've only tried refinishing an old piece of furniture once in my life. It was an old rocking chair I bought at a thrift store. The plan was to strip it down to bare wood and re-stain it. In no time at all I would have this great "new" old rocker. That didn't happen. I never got past the stripping stage. No matter how much I sanded I could not get all the layers of old paint out of the crevices. I was doing it all by hand because I was adamant I would not end up buying $200 worth of tools to refinish a $12 rocker. Frustrated, I re-donated that old chair to the same thrift store I bought it from. It looked so bad they almost wouldn't take it. Lesson learned: It is the prep work before the actual refinishing that takes the most effort.

Like many people, my dream of writing a book for years remained only that—a dream. Then two years ago I came up with the idea of publishing pieces I'd written for my internet blog. Collecting and sorting was a major first step. I reviewed hundreds of posts. Anything which smacked of commentary on (then) current events got cut. Those essays served their usefulness at the time but would be as interesting in book form as yesterday's newspaper.

Once I had a stack of essays selected I had another dilemma. As a writer I was conflicted about editing them. Do I give myself permission to revise them or not? Were they finished works frozen in time? Or were they like rooms in a house all due for a fresh coat of paint and some sprucing up? I read a couple of them and the answer was clear. *Oh yeah; these are definitely getting a fresh coat of paint.*

OK, they really weren't *that* bad. (Well, some were—but I am not telling you which ones.)

Preachers I know often remind each other of the words of Puritan pastor Richard Baxter, "I preached…as a dying man to dying men," encouraging each other to do likewise. Invoking Baxter's words is a charge to be passionate and uncompromisingly clear in preaching the message of Jesus Christ. I wrote this book because in 2005 Jesus Christ changed my life. I wrote this book as a dying man writing to dying men to tell anyone I can about Jesus.

Let me tell you a little of my story. For 20 years I thought I was Christian. I grew up in New Jersey. I was raised Roman Catholic but left Catholicism at 13 years old. At a Pentecostal church service one night I walked the church aisle and prayed a "Sinner's Prayer." That was the start of my decades-long hypocrisy. I had a working knowledge of the Bible. I argued against liberal, Bible-less Christianity. I wrote evangelistic things and told others about Jesus. I had seasons over those two decades when I was very religious. And I had seasons when I said and did and thought unspeakable, shameful things I wince at today. And that is the problem. I did not wince at them back then. Looking back I had no true brokenness over my sins so how could I possibly really understand the great sacrifice Jesus made to take the

Pleasant Places

punishment for them? My life had no genuine evidence I was ever truly saved. But I'm getting ahead of myself.

I explain the Christian doctrine of sanctification (spiritual maturing) as looking like a long term stock market chart. Yes there are down times when trials or disciplines come, but the long-term "chart" of a healthy Christian's life shows a smooth upward progression. Those down times aren't as noticeable in the overall picture. What is noticeable is growing trust in and obedience to the Lord coupled with a deepening desire to avoid sin.

The chart of my life from 13 to 34 showed I was spiritual mess who had no consistency in my faith at all. For awhile I would be a super-Christian spiking high listening to Keith Green and studying my Bible daily. Eventually the crash would come and I would drop off for months at a time.

After high school my brother got me a job at a software company. There I met the woman I would marry a year later. I was only 20 years old. My parents advised against it. Her parents advised against it. The associate pastor of the church I had stopped going to advised against it. No one was particularly surprised when we eloped. We both professed to be Christians but I was not a godly husband and she was not a godly wife. Thirteen years later, in 2004, we divorced.

No single event caused the death of our marriage. It was on life support for a long time anyway. Ironically, just the month before things fell apart we had joined a church together. It was a rock-solid, Bible teaching church. I started attending a men's group one morning each week before work. Things seemed right. Over the early months of 2004 things got worse though instead of better. Even the Christian marriage counselor we went to was blunt when he said it would take a "miracle" to save our marriage.

That miracle never happened.

I grew furious with God. I had prayed and fasted but by April and May I was crushed. Why would he allow our marriage to disintegrate like this? Why was God ignoring my cries for help? I decided everything about God was a lie. The leadership at the church we were at was no help at all. In fact, they made things worse. To this day I believe it is a good church. I would recommend it to someone looking for a church home. I just think the pastors and elders who were involved in our situation could have handled things better.

With nowhere else to turn—not God, not church—I resolved to go it alone. I thumbed my nose at God, left the church, and began a rigorous course of self-help humanism. Stress caused me to lose the first ten pounds but I capitalized on the opportunity and dropped a total of 30 pounds. I began to eat and exercise with the zeal of a world-class athlete. I ran a mile faster than I did in high school. I was in the best physical shape of my life, even if my finances were not.

The financial arrangement imposed by the divorce judge was awful. I was a successful Information Technology professional making good money but what the judge ordered me to pay as temporary alimony left me functionally broke each month. Looking back, I am filled with thanks and praise to God that it was, in fact, temporary. (We had no children, so that also streamlined the proceedings.) Insult, as the saying goes, was added to injury because I also had to pay my lawyer.

Pleasant Places

Little by little life went on. From the spring of 2004 until September 2005 life as a man in the throes of divorce and starting over was a mixed bag. My employer offered me an opportunity to take a company-paid transfer to supervise a team in Tampa, Florida. I was single (emotionally, if not legally at first), and in the sunshine capital of the world. And by then the temporary alimony arrangement was over and I was a free man with pocket money to spend. I traded my pickup truck and Georgia for a convertible sports car and Florida's sun and fun. I ate at good restaurants, met new people, enjoyed my new apartment, and all the things that go with starting a new life (and one without God).

Much like the Prodigal Son, what started out great did not last. Inside I grew miserable I tried different techniques to cope but was plagued by guilt and panic attacks. I had guilt for how I was living, guilt for how I was dishonoring those I loved, and then panic attacks because of the guilt. But I also was asking myself over and over: *What am I going to do with my life?* Outside I was the epitome of a Type-A success. Inside I was a wreck. And that is how Jesus stepped in.

On September 15, 2005 I was anxious and tense—in other words it was an ordinary day. My girlfriend came over after work. Once again she saw me consumed by anxiety she could not understand. I had gone back to church once a few weeks before and tried to talk her into bringing God into our relationship but she, being an atheist, had no interest in God. Inside I felt I had no choice. I broke down and said that I wasn't sure what it was supposed to look like but that I needed to go back to God. The night collapsed and so did our relationship. She left saying she needed time apart for a while. Feeling totally alone in the world, all I could do was weep in my one bedroom apartment.

I would cry a lot more over the next weeks and months, but that night I cried out to Jesus to save me. I confessed every sin I could think of, as far back as I could think of. I wept over my sin. I wept over my failed marriage. I wept over the relationship that just walked out my door and probably wasn't coming back. I wept over how I'd hurt people I loved. Ultimately I wept because God was breaking me. He had to because all along it was his gracious desire to rebuild me. What he had to work with was beyond repair. Sin has ruined all of us that way. He had to break me to pieces and start over his way. Jesus put it another way when he said, "New wine has to be put into fresh [new] wineskins" (Luke 5:38).

My life since that day has never been the same. I am not saying it happens to everyone, but within a couple of days my guilt and my panic attacks stopped. Like the untamed wind and churning waves Jesus commanded to "Be still!" there on the Sea of Galilee, the constant chatter of busy, anxious thoughts inside me were silenced. Next God led me to a church. I enrolled in the DivorceCare[2] ministry they had just started and learned fundamental life skills as a divorced person and as a Christian. And it was there he also brought me to brothers and sisters in Christ.

As he healed me and made me a new person, God also brought someone very special into my life. I met Amy in the singles Bible study at church. I know what you are thinking: *Singles Bible study, huh?* Well, before you snicker or roll your

---

[2] http://www.divorcecare.org

Pleasant Places

eyes: This was a group of only a dozen adults, most of them retirees. God knew what he was doing; it was as safe a singles group as it sounds.

By March of 2006, over lunch at Mel's Hot Dogs, Amy and I nervously agreed that, yes, whatever we had been doing together for the past several months probably was technically "dating." Thankfully we were both more sure of ourselves and each other when we exchanged wedding vows a year later.

I think it is worth pausing here to address the issue of remarriage. A lot can be said about the topic of Christians and remarriage, more than can be mentioned here. I took the question of whether it was right for me to remarry seriously. Any man or woman who has divorce in his or her past, yet truly desires to follow the Lord above all else, will wrestle with this question eventually. After much prayer and Bible study, I concluded that as long as Amy and I kept the Lord first in our relationship, including ahead of our own desire to be married, we were in his will to move forward. And if he guided us otherwise, we would obey. This time, too, I was committed to do it right—Amy and I were middle-aged adults, but I still asked both sets of parents for their blessing first. We also completed a pre-engagement/pre-marital counseling program with our pastor. Surrounded by friends and family, we sealed the deal April 28, 2007.

And what God has done since then has been a joy. Yes, there have been times of tragedy and hardship and trial. Through it all God has been so good. And that is why I want to tell anyone I can. Even if they had to give up everything they own and everything they are in this world, Jesus is worth it all.

Thank you for the privilege of having my words in your hands. We're all busy and yet you are graciously sharing your time with me. I am honored. I promise you that I took more care and effort on each word you read than I did on that thrift store rocker! But seriously, I had to. For one day I will stand before God and give account for what I offer you in these pages. I want you to have as much helpful, solid truth as I can hope to write.

Sometimes life is hard. But like David wrote in Psalm 16, in the difficult times we can remember how the Lord has been so good to us. He holds our lot; our boundary lines have fallen to us in pleasant places. The most important thing we can live our life for is to know and serve the Lord Jesus Christ. I hope and pray you are encouraged, inspired, and yes, maybe even a little stung by what is in this book. May God use all of it to bring himself glory through your life and mine. And may you be refreshed to say with David,

"The lines have fallen for me in pleasant places;
indeed, I have a beautiful inheritance."

To God be the glory,

Anthony Russo
January 15, 2014

Pleasant Places

DID GOD BUY YOUR LUNCH OR SAVE YOU FROM CHOKING?

Imagine one day you and I have lunch together. When the check comes you smile and reach for it, "This one's on me."

"Hey, thanks!" And as I drove away I would think that was a pleasant surprise. But let's be honest. It was just lunch. Maybe my share of the bill cost you ten or twelve dollars. Not a big deal. I might remember to tell my wife about your kindness by the time I got home, or I might not. Or I might forget all about it a mile down the road. If I'm thoughtful, I might make a mental note to reciprocate the next time we get together, but that's about it. Eventually I would forget that you bought me lunch. Life would go on. It would be strange if I went around telling everyone I met what great a person you were for what you did. After all, you only bought my lunch, right?

Change the story. Now imagine that same lunch together, only this time I start choking. Tears begin to stream down my reddening face. I wave my hands frantically, hoping you understand what is happening. My life is flashing before my eyes. All I see are the fearful faces of other patrons staring helplessly at me. Some don't even know and keep on eating and talking and laughing. Meanwhile terror has overwhelmed me. Airless agony grips me. I hear myself try to cough with what little air I am getting, but it isn't enough. I want to scream but all I can manage is a sickening sort of gurgle as my neck muscles uncontrollably lock hard around what is lodged in my throat, trying to do something with it. My eyes are filled with panic. The fear on my face says it all: *Save me!*

Then, with complete control of the situation, you come around the table and get behind me. Making a fist with one hand, you wedge it hard into my abdomen and cover it with your other hand. "Try to relax!" With all your power you heave a jolting Heimlich thrust up and into my midsection. It didn't work! I feel my life slipping away. The horror of the moment terrifies me. *DEAR GOD, HELP ME!*

Another thrust. My stomach aches like it just got kicked with a steel-toed boot. A loud, sickening pop reverberates in my head as my throat burns from the slicing pain of what just got forced out. The whole restaurant now is fixed on me as my body spasms to inhale into my lungs all the air it can. Coughing uncontrollably, with one hand I reach for a napkin to wipe my mouth and with the other give a wave that I'm all right. The deep red-blue color in my face recedes to normal and for the first time I realize...

I'm going to live. I'M GOING TO LIVE!

I am going to live and I have you to thank. *You* saved my life! I was as good as dead and you saved me. Thank you! Thank you! From that moment I am forever indebted to you. You could never ask anything too much of me anymore because I am wholly indebted to you for saving my life. I would never stop being grateful to you. I would never forget what you did. I would want to tell everyone who would listen about how you saved me.

Now, be honest: Where do you see yourself in this story? Better yet, where do you see God? Do you live life as though God only bought your lunch? You may say "Oh, no, certainly not." But then what do your actions say? Does the disconnect between your words and your actions expose the truth that all you've done is wink at God, as if to give him the thumbs-up and say, "Thanks God, I'll getcha back next time," and you go on with your life? You wouldn't be the only one. That is the attitude of most of what passes for Christianity in America and around the world these days. It was my attitude for over 20 years. It is the attitude of the 99 out of 100 people on the street who, if asked, would claim to be Christian. If your view of God is that low, that trite, let me strongly suggest to you that you probably don't know him at all. Until we embrace the Lord as one who has ransomed us from death—undeservedly so, mind you—we regard God with about as much honor and gratitude as if he'd only spent a few dollars and bought us a free lunch.

The Gospel of Jesus Christ is infinitely more than a story about God's free lunch generosity. It is about the Son of God being holy, sinless, perfect and glorious and each of us being sinful ungrateful rebels bent on disobedience and completely deserving of eternal punishment as proper payment as a result. But the Good News is that Jesus suffered, nailed to a cross at the hands of his own creation, bore the full measure of God the Father's wrath that was stored up and waiting for us. We deserve death but Jesus died in our place. We deserve hell but God the Father extends us mercy and forgiveness through the righteousness of his Son. The only proper response is, as Paul said in Romans 12:1:

> I appeal to you therefore, brothers, by the mercies of God, to present your bodies as a living sacrifice, holy and acceptable to God, which is your spiritual worship.

I know my illustration above isn't perfect. But the point is still valid. Unless we see ourselves as utterly, helplessly doomed in our sin we don't see Jesus mighty to save us—so how can we really be grateful for what he did? And that means we miss what it really means to be a Christian. Unless our lives are transformed by an all-surrendering awe of him because he saved us, we have no part in him. Only when we understand the Gospel rightly are we willing to do whatever he asks of us. And our enthusiasm and loyalty are not to try to pay back (we know we never could), they only demonstrate the love and gratitude we have for rescuing us.

So let me ask you: Did God buy your lunch or save you from choking?

Everything Seemingly is Spinning Out of Control

That was the headline of the Associated Press article a few years back. The article surveyed the American landscape of politics, the economy, natural disasters, sports and entertainment to look for hope but found little. It tried to end positively, talking about the historical rebounds which always followed previous times of uncertainty. The writer wondered, "maybe this is what the 21st century will be about—a great unraveling of some things long taken for granted."[3]

Living as believers, we demonstrate our trust in a sovereign God before a world that is fragile and frightened. We look beyond the headlines. We look instead to "Jesus, the founder and perfecter of our faith" (Hebrews 12:2). When our hearts are set on him he promises peace—even joy—despite the despair that surrounds us. Jesus reassures us we will have hardship and tribulation in the world. "But take heart," he says, "I have overcome the world" (John 16:33). In his second letter to the church at Corinth Paul described his situation this way:

> We are afflicted in every way, but not crushed; perplexed, but not driven to despair, persecuted, but not forsaken; struck down, but not destroyed...we do not lose heart" (2 Corinthians 4:8,9,16a).

---

[3] http://news.yahoo.com/s/ap/20080621/ap_on_re_us/out_of_control as of June, 2008.

Anthony F. Russo

In the early 1940s Japan almost conquered China. The Japanese army moved swiftly and cruelly across the land. Two hundred miles northwest of Hong Kong, in the city of Wuchow, a young Southern Baptist missionary doctor, Bill Wallace, was the chief surgeon and administrator of the mission hospital. As the bombings and aerial machine-gun attacks worsened, Wuchow fell. Wallace orchestrated the evacuation of the hospital, then led 50 doctors, nurses, and staff on what became a year-long odyssey to other cities. The roving hospital—they had taken all their equipment and medicines and setup camp wherever they went—faced innumerable diseases, air raids, shortages, and the deaths two team members during the war-ravaged time. It was only the fall of Japan at V-J Day in 1945 that finally brought relief and allowed for a return to Wuchow. As they sailed into view of Wuchow, the entire group burst into a chorus of praise to Jesus singing that great, triumphant hymn, *Crown Him with Many Crowns*.

Christians are not inoculated against sometimes feeling everything is "spinning out of control." The difference, however, is that in those times we draw comfort from the One who is always in control, "the Lamb upon his throne."

Pleasant Places

IF A MISSIONARY CAME TO AMERICA

Strictly speaking, one does not have to *go* to be a missionary. Distance is irrelevant. Every Christian is called to think, act, and be a missionary right where they are. In America, where I live, we have a great deal more freedoms than in other parts of the world where Christians are spreading the Gospel. We can open-air preach, pass out tracts, worship publicly and meet privately. But even with all these liberties, I wonder what opportunities we are missing?

This got me thinking, *What if a missionary came to America?*

What evangelistic efforts would they undertake? How would a missionary to Anytown, USA plant a church? Would they go door to door? Would they walk the streets and pass out tracts? How would missions efforts to rural areas differ from those within cities? Yes, I know American ministries have their methods but I am curious about an outsider's perspective. If a missionary came to America what opportunities would they see in plain sight which we overlook? Surely they would see far more potential (and far more need) than we do. In fact, as offensive as it may sound, they would likely want to start within the church, not outside it.

It is sad to think this country that financially supports and sends missionaries all over the world could use a missionary endeavor on its own soil. But think about it. We super-size our churches but have no room for Jesus inside. It's easy to find the activity center or the coffee shop, but the prayer room is, uh, somewhere down the back hallway. Worse, we amen the TV preachers who promise the financial blessing we want but curse the suggestion that maybe God wants us to be poor or sick or both so he can make us more Christ-like through our suffering. The American version of Christianity is, shall we say, complicated. We'll drive around town for three hours on Saturday carting our kids to every activity under the sun but don't hassle us to drive ten minutes to church on Sunday. That's too far and we're too tired. Besides, we have work tomorrow. You don't expect us to waste all day in church, do you?

In my experience many Americans who profess to be Christians are also quick to boast that they are members at some church and have been for years. They just never go. "I don't have to go to a building to worship God," they say. "I do it in my heart, at home," as if it were up to them to decide how God is to be worshiped, rather than God himself.

If a missionary came to America I hope he or she would call us out on our Bible reading too. Many of us who claim to be Christian are virtually illiterate when it comes to the Bible. It's no wonder. If I put a dollar in a jar for every dried out, yellowed, beat up Bible I have seen stuffed in the back window of somebody's car, I could tour the Holy Land. Others of us do at least read our Bible. Sometimes. We'll read the random page we open to and get our quick fix—unless whatever it says doesn't fit the message we think God has for us. Then we flip to something else. Or close the book and find our answer in that other way God apparently now talks to us: Facebook.

I know I sound severe, but there is hope. If a missionary came to America there are tens of thousands of God's

Pleasant Places

people who would join the Gospel awakening. The Lord Jesus has many who love him in cities and towns all over the country. Every moment of every day somewhere in the United States a song of praise rises to heaven. But why wait for God to send help from abroad? Let's be asking God to give us eyes to see our churches, our neighbors, our cities and our towns in a new way. Instead of asking *What if a missionary came to America?* Let's be that missionary, even if it means first calling ourselves to repentance.

THE SWORD AND THE HANDRAIL

I am often reminded in things I read that life sometimes calls for swift and severe action. When we grow lazy in our prayer life we need to lunge at our lethargy and wrestle it into submission. We have every right to march that lying feeling that God doesn't love us, or hasn't forgiven us, right out the door. Every child of God has days when they simply don't "feel" like reading the Bible; those days are best met head-on and Bible open. (Incidentally, this can happen naturally because we are overly familiar with whatever Bible story we are reading that day. Try reading from a different translation, or seek out variety by reading from the Psalms instead.)

The Bible is full of examples of swift action. Lot fled Sodom before its destruction. The Israelite midwives knew better than to follow Pharaoh's orders to kill the male babies. Their quick thinking saved lives. Paul told Timothy to "flee youthful passions and pursue righteousness, faith, love, and peace" (2 Timothy 2:22). Dozens more examples from Scripture can be given.

The situations God teaches us to confront aren't only spiritual ones either. Sometimes it is our selfishness that requires discipline, like when I see the kitchen trash needs to go out but my first thought is to leave it for my wife to do. God uses the ordinary circumstances of life to point out our sinfully short temper in line, on hold, behind the wheel, or with *that* coworker. For those moments when the dead man of our old self comes alive (see Ephesians 4:17-27), it is good to know how to handle a sword (Ephesians 6).

We are saved by grace alone and without Jesus we can do nothing (John 15:5), but self-discipline is essential in a

Pleasant Places

Christian's life. Jesus told us in a vivid metaphor it would be better to cut off our hand or gouge out our own eye if either is causing us to sin. Paul said he trained his body like an athlete does, beating it into submission. Job made a covenant with his eyes not to gaze longingly on a woman (Job 31:1). But self-discipline will only take us so far. We would be nothing more than humanists if all we relied on was sheer will power. And we'd surely fail. Paul said he was able to be content in every circumstance because it was Christ who made it possible (Philippians 4:13).

But what about when we don't have the strength to fight? What if we are tired? What if the spirit really is willing but the flesh is proving its weakness? (Matthew 26:41; Mark 14:38). What if we know the right thing to do but we stayed up all night with a sick child or yesterday's chemo treatment is getting the best of us again? And some days deep down we think we are failures because we cannot cajole ourselves to do better.

That is not the Gospel. Remember Paul's words to the Galatians? "Are you so foolish? Having begun by the Spirit, are you now being perfected by the flesh?" (Galatians 3:3). Our heavenly Father loves us. Many times I have leaned on the comforting words of Psalm 103:13-14,

> As a father shows compassion to his children, so the Lord shows compassion to those who fear him. For he knows our frame; he remembers that we are dust.

There is no shame in acknowledging our helplessness to the Lord. Quite the opposite! Jesus is our Friend. "A bruised reed he will not break, and a faintly burning wick he will not quench" (Isaiah 42:3). He will only embrace us in his strong arms and carry us through if we tell him plainly,

> *Lord, I am dreading the day ahead. I already have a hundred thoughts and the To-Do list in my head is growing with every passing minute as I think of more and more that needs to be done today. I know this time is important. I know it is important for me to spend time with you and to sit at your feet and to hear from you through your word.*

And in those aching, sorrowful times when are too weak to even call out to him, the Lord has already assured us of his mercy,

> Likewise the Spirit helps us in our weakness. For we do not know what to pray for as we ought, but the Spirit himself intercedes for us with groanings too deep for words (Romans 8:26)

Some days we wield the sword. Some days we hold the handrail. The lesson for us is always the same, trust in the Lord.

> *O to grace how great a debtor*
> *daily I'm constrained to be!*
> *Let thy goodness, like a fetter,*
> *bind my wandering heart to thee.*
> *Prone to wander, Lord, I feel it,*
> *prone to leave the God I love;*
> *here's my heart, O take and seal it,*
> *seal it for thy courts above.*
>
> *-"Come Thou Fount of Every Blessing"*
> *Words by Robert Robinson*

HE WALKS AMONG THE LAMPSTANDS

I've been thinking a lot about the first three chapters of Revelation, particularly Jesus' comments to each of the seven churches. He begins by revealing an attribute of himself to each church. To Ephesus, for example, he is the One "who holds the seven stars in his right hand, who walks among the seven golden lampstands" (Revelation 2:1). Then he reminds each of them, "I know..." as in I know your works…, where you live, your reputation, etc. With some differences, Jesus usually tells them their particular fault(s) a verse or two later, "...nevertheless I have this against you..." followed by a prescription of how to rectify the divine grievance. Jesus, of course, knows exactly what is going on in his churches.

I know the whole word of God is written to me for my instruction (2 Timothy 3:16) but I've been asking the Lord to show me what he sees in me like he showed each of the churches. In Revelation 2:23, Jesus reminds us, "I am he who searches the minds and hearts." If Jesus dictated a letter to me like he did them, what would follow, "I know your works..."? What would follow, "...nevertheless I have this against you..."? In what areas do I need to repent?

Jesus still walks among the lampstands of his churches today. What would he say about yours? About you? Let's be sure we are living faithfully.

Anthony F. Russo

The Day I Learned I Could Do More

Note: The following appeared as a blog post on the independent blog of Southern Baptist writers SBCvoices.com January 28, 2011 Some grammatical edits have been made.-AR

[In January 2011] I wrote a short article wishing I could do more to end abortion. I said that my voice "just seems so small and insignificant" compared to the need. A friend who has been a long-time pro-life advocate and is well connected in the pro-life movement saw my post and challenged me: I could, in fact, do more.

This morning I went with him to a local abortion clinic. There was no picketing, no carrying signs. No one jeered at, maligned, or otherwise harassed the women who went in to end the lives of their unborn babies. We stayed the legal distance away and never once obstructed their pathway.

Then we prayed. We prayed for them, for their babies, and for the workers inside. Next, we pleaded. Earnestly. We pleaded with the women and their friends to please, please delay their decision and let us get them alternative help. Then we preached the Gospel.

No one called down coals of fire and damnation on them or called them names. We preached Christ and him crucified. We did not sugar-coat or suppress the truth: What they were engaging in was nothing less than murder; God would not hold them guiltless. Yet if they would turn to him and ask his forgiveness he come swiftly to their side with pardon and healing. Our final words before we left were, "We love you."

Pleasant Places

You must understand: I have never done this sort of thing before. Today I stood face-to-face with another human being and pleaded with them to not kill someone. I can't begin to explain the force of that intimate human connection.

What, you ask, were the results? Only God knows. I can tell you that no one complained or cursed. Mostly we were ignored (I'm told this is not always the case).

I learned a lot today. I learned that I could, in fact, do more. All of us can. Did you know that just standing your legal ground on the sidewalk is sometimes enough of a visual deterrent? Not that we swagger and look imposing (I'm 5'7" and academic looking…I'm about as imposing as bread dough), rather, people think "Oh, nevermind, I'll come back another day."

And really, that is a small victory in itself. That baby gets another day.

Lost and Found

I once got lost in the woods. I think it was February 2004. I was living in Atlanta back then. In the early stages of the failure of my first marriage I thought a night away in a mountain cabin up in North Georgia would clear my head and help me think. I left after work and arrived with enough daylight left to walk before cooking dinner. The plan was to follow the short trail the cabin owner told me about that went from my cabin, up along the ridgeline, and turn around at the sign he warned me turn around at; I'd be there and back within 30 minutes. Since I was up there to relax I left my cell phone in the cabin—*I wouldn't need it anyway*.

(Did I mention I'm from New Jersey? Malls I know. Diners I know. The only "hiking" I did as a kid was to the convenience store to get junk food.)

There was No Sign

I never saw the sign. To this day I still believe it was either not there or covered over by leaves. I started to think I'd gone too far. I turned around to go back but then turned around again because I wasn't sure. That's when I noticed the trail was covered with fallen leaves and everywhere I looked looked exactly the same. I was lost.

I didn't plan on telling the whole story about being lost in the woods. Kind of like what happened that day, I'm too far in turn back now. As I wandered in the woods trying to find my way back, I had the idea of ripping off my shirt pocket and tearing it into strips. I tied a few strips at eye level on branches along the way in case I needed to retrace my steps or others looked for me the next day. And I found a stream.

Pleasant Places

I learned later that the temperatures were down in the 50s. All I had was a light sweatshirt and it wasn't doing much good.

STAY OR GO

In the last rays of daylight I found shelter under a large fallen tree. My thought was I would sleep there for the night and see what tomorrow held. As I lay curled within the tree trunk I was kind of proud of my idea of using strips of shirt, for finding water, and for being smart enough to use the tree trunk for shelter (completely missing the fact that I caused myself to get lost in the first place). That's when I heard a low growling sound that sounded like it was coming from uphill. I knew the area had bear. I hoped this one didn't find my scent. I heard it again. I thought about making a run for it. That's when I realized the growl wasn't coming from uphill but from my hungry stomach.

After a while I realized staying under the trunk of a tree somewhere in the mountains was not worth the anxiety of wondering about real bears or other things with claws and sharp teeth. I decided to follow the stream and take my chances. There was dog barking over a distant ridge. Maybe on the other side was somebody's house.

FOUND

About four hours later, including crawling in the night along that stream by moonlight, I walked to a place where I heard the cabin owner and the ranger and then saw their flashlights searching in the direction of my voice. Ironically, the cabin owner forgot to have me sign some disclaimer form. When he got to my cabin and found it unlocked and my keys, wallet, and cell phone on the table along with my bag of food, he knew I must've gotten lost so he called the ranger. Safely back at my cabin a short time later, I had more to think about than when I arrived.

Lessons Learned

I know now that the Lord was definitely watching out for me. I was fine the whole time and never really in any danger. I learned after that I made the mistake experts warn of: In the first minutes of a sudden crisis it is crucial to resist the natural urge to panic. I also learned that, despite getting myself lost, with no training or experience I did OK taking care of myself out there. Believe it or not, many times since God has used the experience to remind me that (humanly speaking) I can do more than I think I can. And most importantly, he got me through that, so I know he'll get me through everything else in life.

Pleasant Places

TROUBLE READING THROUGH LEVITICUS? KNOW THE THREE C'S

Some Christians avoid the Old Testament. They feel as lost in the Bible as I did in the North Georgia Mountains. For them it is unfamiliar territory. When I talk to some people about reading the Bible, one response I get is that the person started reading in Genesis, but gave up by Leviticus, only two books later. I'm reading Leviticus now in my own Bible reading plan, so I think about those folks as I make my way through it. It can be a bewildering landscape if you have no idea what you are reading, or why it is in the Bible. There are three ideas I keep in mind when I read Leviticus:

CONTEXT

Consider the context of the book. Here are over a million people who, until recently, were slaves in Egypt for over four hundred years. By God's mighty hand they have been delivered out of Pharaoh's cruel Egypt. Famously safe on the other side of the Red Sea, God leads them into the Sinai wilderness, en-route to the Promised Land. The children of Israel are learning to live not just on their own, but as new nation literally and miraculously birthed out of another and specially chosen to live as God's chosen people. Leviticus is a book of laying down crucial ground rules and learning to follow the Lord.

CONSECRATION

While there are a lot of rules and regulations presented to the priests and the people, they signify something more: Being wholly devoted to the Lord. That is the intent behind the word "holy." It means to be consecrated, set apart. Every other nation around the Israelites was steeped in pagan idolatry. Every other nation on earth had veered hard away from God (really ever since Genesis chapter three). But God was doing a work, a much bigger work than they knew. They were to be wholly devoted to him. Impurity, idolatry, and iniquity were not going to be tolerated. Israel was to be wholly holy. They were to be the special, chosen, representative people of Yahweh. Yet, God knew they would sin. In his mercy he prescribed the means to seek forgiveness for their sins, which brings us to...

CHRIST

In Leviticus chapter 9 we see the first animal slaughtered for the sins of the people under these new rules of priestly intervention and atonement (hence the term "Levitical priesthood"). Over the next thousand-plus years millions of animals would be slaughtered to atone for the sins of the people. Yet none of those sacrifices, individually or all together, could truly take away the sins of the people. To use the question from the old hymn, "What can wash away my sin?"

The answer in the song is the answer of the Scriptures: Nothing but the blood of Jesus. All the sacrifices pointed in vivid picture form to the one great sacrifice that would one day come. Jesus, the Lord himself, as "the Lamb of God who takes away the sins of the world" would be the perfect one-for-all sacrifice for sin for those who would be saved from their just punishment.

R.C. Sproul tells the story of when he first started teaching the Bible as a college professor. Students would say to him, "Oh, Professor Sproul, you make the Bible come alive for

Pleasant Places

me!" Aware that they were trying to compliment him, he refuted their words. "Look, I can't make the Bible come alive, because I can't make anything come alive that already *is* alive!" He said to them, "There's nothing wrong with sacred Scripture. What you're noticing with my animation and my excitement is my response to the Scriptures… The Bible makes me come alive, rather than my making the Bible come alive!"[4]

That is a great testimony to the value of studying the Bible. Regular Bible reading and study literally is walking alongside God. The Holy Spirit knows the way and delights to lead us. When we follow him he points out all the beauty and truth along the way.

---

[4] R.C. Sproul, *Dust to Glory*, Session 1, Creation.

Anthony F. Russo

A Month of Blessings:
Benefits of Being a Christian

I was thinking last week of blessings that come as a result of Christmas. And by "Christmas" I mean that as a shorthand word referring to Jesus' entire birth, life, ministry, death, resurrection, ascension, future return and eternal reign. There are infinitely more than we can ever assemble; in the Person of the Lord alone there are endless treasures to delight in. In no time at all I came up with over 30 benefits we receive when we are born again as believers in Jesus Christ.

Included with each benefit are a few supporting Scriptures. For most, more can be referenced both in the Old and New and in just considering the full scope of Scripture. Consider using these devotionally. For each day read the Christian benefit, look up the verse(s), think about how it applies in your life and then thank and praise God for each, afterall…

> Bless the Lord, O my soul,
>   and forget not all his benefits,
> who forgives all your iniquity,
>   who heals all your diseases,
> who redeems your life from the pit,
>   who crowns you with steadfast love and mercy,
> who satisfies you with good
>   so that your youth is renewed like the eagle's.
>   (Psalm 103:2-5)

1. Everlasting, free, pardoned life (John 10:10)
2. Full heir of salvation; joint-heir with Christ (Romans 8:17; Galatians 4:7)
3. Peace with God our Creator (Romans 5:1; Col 1:20)

Pleasant Places

4. Adopted as a child of God (Romans 8; Galatians 4:5; Ephesians 1:5)
5. Once our enemy, God becomes our Friend and Father (Colossians 1:19-23)
6. Truth—in this confusing world we have God's word (John 8:32, 14:6, 17:17)
    7. The indwelling of the Holy Spirit (2 Corinthians 5:5; Galatians 4:6)
8. Christ in us, the hope of glory (Colossians 1:27)
9. Love replaces hate—we have love for our fellow man (Romans 5:5; 1 John 3:18)
10. Freedom—chains of addiction to alcohol, sex, pornography, drugs, whatever—Jesus unshackles our hands, setting us free forever (John 8:36)
11. Comfort in sorrows (Psalm 23:4; 2 Corinthians 1:3, 4)
12. Hope in the midst of grief (Psalm 30:5)
13. Joy the world does not and cannot know (1 Peter 1:8)
14. Peace beyond understanding (Philippians 4:7)
15. The privileges of prayer & worship (Psalm 150; Hebrews 4:16)
16. Forgiveness of all our sins (Psalm 103:12; Isaiah 1:18)
17. All our dark regrets dealt with on the cross (Ephesians 1, 2)
18. Baptism (Romans 6:4; Ephesians 4:5; Colossians 2:12)
19. The Lord's Supper (John 17; 1 Corinthians 11:24-34)
20. Membership into the worldwide, eternal Church (1 Corinthians 12:12-27; Hebrews 12:22-24; Revelation 5:9,10)
21. Jesus, as High Priest, interceding for us (Romans 8:34; Ephesians 3:12; Hebrews 4:16; Hebrews 7)
22. Heaven—Eternity with God, our Savior (Revelation 21, 22)

23. Heaven—Reunion with believing friends, loved ones, and people from every culture, time, language in history (Revelation 5:9, 10)
24. A new name promised to you, one known only to you and the Lord (Revelation 2:17, 3:12)
25. The Holy Spirit in us, completing us and fitting us for heaven (2 Corinthians 1:22, 5:5; Ephesians 1:14, 4:30)
26. Justified before God (Romans 5, 8:1-4)
27. Sanctified: Anointed with the blood of Jesus, made holy and fit for service to the Lord (Romans 6:9-11)
28. The promise of resurrection (John 11:24-26; Romans 6:1-11)
29. The promise of glory: Risen, reigning with Christ, glorified with a new, perfect body (1 Corinthians 15:51,52; 2 Corinthians 4:17)
30. Eternal life—all of this starts the moment we surrender to Jesus and it never, ever stops (John 3:16; 1 Thessalonians 4:16-18)
31. Hope, now and forever. Real hope, resting in God who always keeps his word (Romans 8:18-25, 15:4; 1 Thessalonians 5:24)

Every day is a reason to praise the Lord! What other benefits can you think of?

Pleasant Places

Happy Birthday Miss Fleeda

Last night a handful of folks from church went to a nursing home to stage a little surprise birthday party for a sweet church member, Miss Fleeda, who turned 95 this week. It was a simple affair with a small cake and the sounds of "Happy Birthday" filling the corridor as she was wheeled towards us. We hit our crescendo right on cue as she saw our faces and put it all together. (And right before another resident told us to keep it down.) Then we all told her how much we appreciate her and gathered around to hear stories of her life, some reaching back to before the Great Depression. As she poured over 95 years of memories, a theme emerged in all of her stories. All of them involved a girl, then later a woman, then later a wife, then a mother, and later still a widow who, throughout her life, never stopped following after her Lord Jesus Christ.

I can't imagine a more precious life experience than being in your mid-90s, surrounded by young people and telling them story after story of trusting Jesus What a blessed legacy to leave.

Miss Fleeda never thought she'd live to see 95. Who would? I don't think I'll see it, and longevity runs in my family. My father's father was 87 when he died. My dad is 82 years old and still works part-time, bowls on a league, plays golf, and plays guitar in a community Big Band orchestra. Women live longer than men typically, but only the Lord knows. Maybe I will make 95. My wife might. Maybe you will. This raises an important question.

How can you and I prepare for our 95th birthday? I think the answer is: The same way we get ready for any of them; live life for Jesus Christ. Repent and believe the amazing Good News of forgiveness and salvation he offers. Then keep living one day after the next, until the days turn into decades, and we can look back upon a lifetime of grateful, obedient devotion to him.

HE BREAKS OUR CHAINS IN PIECES

> Those who sat in darkness and in the shadow of death, Bound in affliction and irons—they cried out to the Lord in their trouble, and he saved them out of their distresses. He brought them out of the darkness and the shadow of death, and broke their chains in pieces (Psalm 107:10, 13, 14).

Recently I met a computer security expert who also enjoys lock-picking. When he speaks at security conferences he demonstrates how easy it is to pick any lock. All it takes is the right tools and a little finesse. A master locksmith can pick a lock in a few seconds—if even that long!

Psalm 107 describes the people as chained in darkness and death, "[b]ound in affliction and irons." But notice how God delivered them. He did not delicately pick the lock of their chains. I love what the Psalmist says instead. He rejoices that God, "broke their chains in pieces." The Almighty God triumphed in delivering his people, thundering forth in glory and power.

This verse also proclaims the great victory that was won by Jesus on the cross of Calvary. While the world looked on in disgust, laughing in their scorn and rejection, Jesus brought liberty and victory when he proclaimed, "It is finished."

What does this victory look like in the world today? Is this power available for us? Yes! The moment a sinner repents and turns to him for mercy the Lord utterly destroys the chains holding him captive. Jesus Christ has been freeing men and women from their chains of rage, violence, drunkenness, addiction, lust, cursing, lying, sexual immorality, stealing, murder—you name it—for two thousand years. The chains of darkness and despair are no match for the Son of God who alone can boast, "if the Son sets you free, you will be free indeed" (John 8:36).

How appropriate that in the next verse of Psalm 107 the writer says, "Oh that men would give thanks to the Lord for his goodness, and for his wonderful works to the children of men!"

HE REALLY WILL

Life is described with many metaphors. Jesus spoke of life as the narrow road that leads to life eternal. I remember a popular song from the 1990s, "Life is a Highway." Life has been called a game, a journey, an adventure, a dream, and a nightmare, a ride, a river, and a rat race...

Today I was reminded of life as a mountain range. Sometimes there are arduous uphill climbs challenging us to the point of exhaustion. Sometimes the downhills are light and leisurely going. Other times they are so steep they give a crushing assault to our knees with each downward step. We joke about being "over the hill," but experience teaches us life is more than a single mountain. Life is a mountain range with all kinds of difficulties along the way.

For the saint who trusts in the Lord, the mountains take on distinct challenges meant to progress us in our sanctification. The children of the Far King are given their training extending high and far across the spiritual Alps of faith. He will see to it that our peaks are sometimes higher, our valleys lower, and our way harder.

My first seminary class was an intensive three-week course in New Testament Greek. It was a 13-week semester of language study in only three weeks. At the end of the first week I had an 'A' average. By the next week I did so badly that my average tanked from an 'A' to an 'F'. By the third week all I hoped to do was average out a 'C' for the course. One day I asked my professor why, no matter how hard I tried, I just wasn't getting it. Why was God letting me fail? I'll never forget his answer.

"Because he loves you."

It took me a long time to understand his answer.

Our Father does all this because he wants to make us "strong and of good courage" like he did with Joshua. He wants to work in us to make us godly and daring like Esther. He wants to make us humble and obedient like Jesus in his earthly ministry (Philippians 2). The Father works in you and me to form in us those same great and godly characteristics we read about in the lives of all the saints in Scripture.

If you feel abandoned somewhere in the arduous uphill of Mount Circumstance know that you are not forgotten. The Lord knows exactly where you are. He sees you from afar and he is right there with you. Jesus fulfilled his promise that he would send the Holy Spirit and not leave us as orphans (John 14:17-18). He will answer. He will provide. He will give you strength and he will guide. He will. He really will.

Pleasant Places

WHAT IS IT TO PRAY IN FAITH?

Some people pray as if God is the servant and they are the master. They think they have the right to tell God what to do or what is best. That is not true prayer. I read somewhere recently, "Prayer is not presumption." There is much wisdom in that statement.

In one of his books on prayer H. Clay Trumbull includes a quotation and then builds his own thoughts around it. In *Personal Prayer: Its Nature and Scope and Illustrative Answers to Prayer* Trumbull writes:

> Faith rests not on prayer, but on God…Faith is more than reason, but is ever reasonable. As Dr. Mark Hopkins expressed it: "Faith takes God at his word, and surely that is reasonable. it is the most reasonable thing in the world to believe that God will do as He has promised." Such reasonable faith is the basis of all proper prayer. [5]

We are not like prophets of Baal on Mount Carmel, and the Lord certainly is not Baal. Pagans work themselves into emotional fits to rouse their god. Idol worshippers grit their teeth to show their eagerness. In vain they did it on that mountain and in vain they do it today. By contrast, our heavenly Father is good. His word assures us he knows our needs before we ask and he cares for us greatly. Jesus told us what he is like when he said,

---

[5] *Personal Prayer: Its Nature and Scope And Illustrative Answers to Prayer*, Fleming H. Revell Company, New York, 1896, 1900, 1915 (two books in one, this from the latter, page 3)

> Look at the birds of the air: they neither sow nor reap nor gather into barns, and yet your heavenly Father feeds them. Are you not of more value than they? (Matthew 6:26)

Romans 8:31 is a verse that really only began to impress itself on me during a season of trials in 2013, "He who did not spare his own Son but gave him up for us all, how will he not also with him graciously give us all things?"

Trumbull and Hopkins have a good word for us. To pray in faith is to humbly ask of our Father, draw comfort from his promises, and long most of all that his will be done.

The Right Perspective Makes All the Difference

Merriam-Webster defines perspective as, "a view of things…in their true relationship or relative importance."[6] One of the simplest things we can do to benefit our prayer lives is to have the right perspective. In Psalm 3:3 David writes, "But you, O Lord, are a shield about me, my glory..." (NKJV). To have the Lord as our glory is to live so passionately God-ward that our very identity is found in him. If we had a lifetime of great achievements, our final wish would be to have none of it remembered, except that we served the Lord. Better yet, we would be happy to be forgotten if it meant that somehow the Lord would receive praise on earth. When John the Baptist saw Jesus' ministry unfold he said, "He must increase, but I must decrease" (John 3:30). He was willing to be nothing that Christ would be everything. The Apostle Paul said he counted everything loss compared to knowing Jesus (Philippians 3:8). These three men had the same perspective—the Lord was their glory.

In another psalm David also says, "But as for me, I will come into your house in the multitude of your mercy: and in your fear will I worship toward your holy temple" (Psalm 5:7, NKJV). This "fear" is not fright. "Fear" in the context here and elsewhere in the Scriptures means "reverence." How else do we explain David joyfully telling of entering into God's house in the "multitude of his mercy"? How can anyone be

---

[6] "Perspective," The Merriam-Webster Dictionary. Springfield, Mass: Merriam-Webster, Inc. 1997.

frightened of the one who showed mercy? (The Apostle John puts it this way in 1 John 4:18, "There is no fear in love, but perfect love casts out fear.")

Every problem in the world today is directly tied to having the wrong spiritual perspective. Wars erupt because men glory in themselves. Haughty men and women sneer at the God of the Bible as they assert their "right" to do as they please. They have no reverence, no godly fear. To have the Lord as our glory and to give him the reverence he is due are the right perspectives to have, regardless of what the world says.

As Christians, losing perspective presents other problems. When we do not feel like praying it is often because our perception of who the Lord is has gotten skewed. We think we can manage on our own. We think he is mad at us. We think he does not care. We (wrongly!) assume he is too busy for us and our problems.

Having the right perspective changes all of that and fuels our prayers. We recall God's sovereignty, holiness, and majesty. We approach his holy temple in reverence. We remember his mercy. We remember his goodness and kindness and faithfulness. We remember his love.

Sometimes we have to remind ourselves of these things. When we remember how we are now reconciled with the Father, joint heirs with Christ and empowered daily by the Spirit, the drudgery of duty is lifted and prayer becomes a joy. The right perspective makes all the difference!

Pleasant Places

THE STAMP HEARD 'ROUND THE WORLD

One dollar and fifteen cents. As of this writing, that's all it costs to mail a standard single-page letter envelope from the United States to many parts of the world. That may not seem like much at all, but what if a stranger on the other side of the planet thought enough to write, print, and mail you a letter of encouragement while you were alone in jail for being a Christian? Would you be that stranger to someone today?

PrisonerAlert.com, a ministry of Voice of the Martyrs, is a website that enables you to create letters to imprisoned believers around the world. After first reading the process and precautions, you pick the person, select the sentences you would like to include in your note, print it, and mail it. In less than 10 minutes you can offer a cup of water as it were to a brother or sister in jail on the other side of the world.

One way you can make your letter unique is to use paper that has pre-printed border, or bright, joyful colors your reader may not see in the confines of a drab prison. Or use an inspiring landscape photo you took somewhere on vacation as the 50% transparent background image behind the text. Who knows what outside view, if any, they see? Pasting the body of the letter into a Microsoft Word document with a neutral, serene background image is a quick way to enhance the letter to make it even more special.

Imagine if you were imprisoned for your faith in Jesus. Imagine how happy you would be if you received a letter. Now imagine how encouraging 10,000 letters from Christians all around the world would be! You can bless someone else by taking the time to be one of those voices of hope.

HEALED...TO SERVE

> Now Simon's mother-in-law lay ill with a fever, and immediately they told him about her. And he came and took her by the hand and lifted her up, and the fever left her, and she began to serve them (Mark 1:30,31).

Every time I read this story it makes me stop. So typical of God's word, two sentences of text give us more wisdom and insight than others could write in a whole book. The Lord healed Peter's mother-in-law and when she rose from her sickbed what did she do? She served them.

This is exactly what God does in the life of every believer. God heals us—actually, raises us from our dead, sinful state—so we can rise and serve. We serve God by serving others, exactly like Scripture shows Peter's mother-in-law doing. It is a beautiful exchange: out of death's uselessness the Spirit of God brings life and usefulness.

What are some things in your life that Jesus healed you from? Drugs? Pornography? Greed? Abuse? One day all whom the Lord has healed from sin and death will be in heaven sharing what he has done, and how he used them. Jesus has healed you to serve. I can't wait to hear your story!

Staying Fixed on Jesus

One day my friend Ed V. at work was teaching me about satellites. I knew nothing about them, but he worked satellite communications in the military. Ed told me there are three main types of satellite orbits around the Earth: NEO, MEO, and GEO. NEO stands for "Near Earth Orbit", these satellites are about 100 miles above the earth and whiz around Earth super-fast, they are only over the same spot for about 10 minutes every hour or so. MEO stands for "Medium Earth Orbit", these satellites are sent farther out away from Earth and generally around the same spot above earth for a somewhat longer time, but still move from that fixed spot. Then there is GEO, or "Geosynchronous Earth Orbit", these satellites are sent a whopping to exactly 23,200 miles out away from Earth's equator. This is roughly three "earths" away from us—*way* out there!

GEO orbiting satellites are sent that far because the earth's gravitational pull is less the farther out an object goes. At exactly that distance an object orbits the earth at the same speed the Earth rotates. What is so significant about that?

A satellite over a fixed spot above the equator will, as the Earth rotates around its axis, be traveling at the same speed. In 24 hours both the Earth and that satellite will be in the same location as a day before. From our perspective on earth that satellite never moves from directly above us.

Now, here is where my mind starts wondering *OK, God can use everything for his purposes, so what is the spiritual application here?* Consider this Bible story:

Pleasant Places

Now as they went on their way, Jesus entered a village. And a woman named Martha welcomed him into her house. And she had a sister called Mary, who sat at the Lord's feet and listened to his teaching. But Martha was distracted with much serving. And she went up to him and said, "Lord, do you not care that my sister has left me to serve alone? Tell her then to help me."

But the Lord answered her, "Martha, Martha, you are anxious and troubled about many things, but one thing is necessary. Mary has chosen the good portion, which will not be taken away from her" (Luke 10:38-42).

How is your "orbit" around the Lord? Are you going at things so fast that you are getting ahead of God? Maybe you are lagging behind what he is doing, way out beyond where you are supposed to be. Our goal in life is to always be at *spiritual 23,200 miles*—the exact place to always stay fixed on him.

Anthony F. Russo

LIFE IN THE THIRD VERSE: IT IS WELL WITH MY SOUL

So many hymns have endearing melodies and powerful, bedrock truths of our "like precious faith" (2 Peter 1:1). There are some hymns which, while I love the whole song, I look forward to getting to a verse that may not be the most familiar one. I have noticed that in most hymns there is great power in the third verse especially. Consider the classic hymn, "It is Well with My Soul" by Horatio Spafford (music by Phillip Bliss). I won't retell the story of the lyrics here, except to say if you are unfamiliar with it I recommend finding it. The third verse says:

> *My sin, Oh, the bliss of this glorious thought!*
> *My sin, not in part but the whole,*
> *Is nailed to the cross, and I bear it no more,*
> *Praise the Lord, praise the Lord, O my soul!*

Can you sing that today? Does your heart share in *the bliss of that glorious thought?* Does this truth lift your soul? Think back on how much Jesus has changed your life since you became a Christian. Think of the bad habits you used to have, the anger, the hatred, the love of sinful pleasures… Remember all the ways you used to try to hide your sin. It never worked, did it? This verse reminds us to celebrate our new birth, the marvelous freedom we now have in Christ, and so to sing with the joy of a sinner set free, *Praise the Lord, praise the Lord, O my soul!*

Pleasant Places

FAITH SETS THE TABLE

Note: This essay was first published as an article in the December 2011, Christian Journal, thechristianjournal.org. –AR

One September evening in 1891, the little North American office-house of the China Inland Mission was especially full. Besides the staff, nearly ten men and women from all across North America were lodging there. Soon these guests would be making the long steamer voyage to join the Mission's famous founder, Dr. Hudson Taylor, as missionaries to China. This day the agency's pantry was empty, except for a little tea and rice. With no food on-hand for dinner and no money to buy any, "Give us this day our daily bread" was the prayer of the hour.

When the director's wife was informed of the dire situation she knew just what to do. Mrs. Frost informed the staff to put a large pot of water on to boil and set the table for dinner. Together they waited on the Lord. Their wait was not long.

Minutes later the housemaid answered the doorbell. She returned to the kitchen with both hands full. A friend of the agency sent a messenger to deliver five partridges with instructions that they would not keep another day and needed to be prepared immediately!

On every page of Scripture we see God richly providing for the needs of his people. When the Israelites were hurried out of Egypt the Bible says, "nor had they prepared provisions for themselves" (Exodus 12:39). God could have told Israel to make provisions for the nearly one million people, plus animals, He was about to lead into the wilderness, but he didn't. He had a better plan. He was going to show them that He would always be their Chief Provision.

In the New Testament our unchanging God is no different. "Your heavenly Father knows that you have need of all these things" is Jesus' comforting reminder to us of God's tender care (Matthew 6:32) From his first miracle of turning to water to wine, to his greatest provision of dying on a cross to pay for our sins and rising from the dead, Jesus showed that God always provides. That's why Paul could later assure the church at Philippi "my God will supply every need of yours according to his riches in glory in Christ Jesus" (Philippians 4:19).

God was Mrs. Frost's Heavenly Father. She, like Paul, knew Him as "my God." When we know and walk with the Lord, we too can be sure that He will always provide. Faith sets the table![7]

---

[7] This story is paraphrased from *By Faith: Henry W. Frost and the China Inland Mission* by Dr. & Mrs. Howard Taylor © 1988 Overseas Missionary Fellowship.

Pleasant Places

LED BY JESUS: A STORY OF REVERENT IMAGINATION

Note: This essay originally titled, "A Memorable Day for a Blind Man." -AR

> And they came to Bethsaida. And some people brought to him a blind man and begged him to touch him. And he took the blind man by the hand and led him out of the village... (Mark 8:22,23).

Oh the love and compassion of Jesus! Imagine the scene: Another day, another city for Jesus and the disciples. This one, like so many, is a busy city and word has gotten out that the Prophet from Nazareth has come to town. By now the scene is a familiar one as the crowd starts forming...and wondering.

What will he do? What will he teach us?

And no doubt the blind man hoped, *Is what they say about this man true? Can he really heal me?*

As he ministers, the "some people" of the text bring the blind man to Jesus. Mark doesn't tell us who they are, but they must have loved the man since he records they "begged" Jesus to touch him. How long had they waited for the Teacher's attention? What might he do?

I can only imagine that with his common, ordinary, human smile, with everyone watching, Jesus does what he has presumably done to others already—he reaches out to touch the man.

But wait, what is he doing?

The Teacher is taking him by the hand. He is walking with him, away from everyone.

Where is he taking him? Where are they going?

And so begins the stroll together away from the crowds and outside the town. For years I read this story and never noticed that detail. Imagine what that moment must have been like! Permit me, please, a moment of reverent imagination…

"Here, take my hand," says Jesus. "Come with me."

"Where are we going, Rabbi?"

"Just outside the village. We'll be right back." And with that the two make their way down the broad thoroughfare. Amidst the sounds of street merchants and children playing Jesus leans in towards the blind man so as to hear and be heard.

"What's your name?"

"David," the man says. His voice is unsure but willing. His feet shuffle cautiously, aware of every subtlety under them.

Jesus is quick to reassure him. "That's a good name!" he says, gently guiding him away from a rock in the road. "Whoa, watch your step there. There you go..." The blind begins to relax and trust, teaching us all a lesson in walking by faith, not sight.

Pleasant Places

As the conversation continues the man realizes they must be outside the town now; the children sound far off. And there beyond the noisy speculation of the crowd, Jesus stops them. You and I return to the inspired Scriptures to read what happens next:

> and when he had spit on his eyes and laid his hands on him, he asked him, "Do you see anything?" And he looked up and said, "I see people, but they look like trees, walking." Then Jesus laid his hands on his eyes again; and he opened his eyes, his sight was restored, and he saw everything clearly. And he sent him to his home, saying, "Do not even enter the village" (Mark 8:23-26).

Even more than Jesus restoring his sight, I wonder if the greater memory for this man was that he walked and talked with Jesus.

Anthony F. Russo

GOD IS YOUR REFUGE

> Trust in him at all times, O people; *pour out your heart before him*; God is a refuge for us (Psalm 62:8, emphasis added).

Think about this: The Lord who holds the universe together, who hears every word and knows the thoughts of the 7+ billion of us on earth each day, *and* of the billions more now in eternity, knows all that is in your heart today.

Before you kneel or sit to spend time with him, he knows. When you are tempted to avoid him out of shame or guilt or grief, he knows. When you feel that what is most heavy upon your heart would be most trivial to him, he knows.

Yet, his invitation to us remains: *pour out your heart before him.* If the slightest matter hinders our complete union with him, the Lord says it is too much. He invites us into an intimate solitude to talk about it. Are you troubled today? *Pour out your heart before him.* He will replace your anxieties with peace. He is our refuge in this world. Believer, the Lord is *your* refuge this day. Hide in him.

Pleasant Places

TWO PLACES IN THIS WORLD

> No one can lose You, my God, unless he forsakes You. And if he forsakes You, where is he to go? If he abandons Your love, his only refuge is Your wrath. - Augustine, *Confessions*, IV, ix

> Enter by the narrow gate; for wide is the gate and broad is the way that leads to destruction, and there are many who go in by it. Because narrow is the gate and difficult is the way which leads to life, and there are few who find it. - Jesus, Matthew 7:13,14

> I am the way, the truth, and the life. No one comes to the Father except through Me. - Jesus, John 14:6

Every person who rejects Jesus as Lord of their life has two witnesses which will testify against him on the day of judgment: His God-given conscience which knows lying, adultery, blasphemy, coveting, stealing, greed, dishonoring God, etc. are wrong, and God's creation all around us that shows us he really does exist, we merely chose to "suppress the truth in unrighteousness" (Romans 1). We have no excuse for our choices and actions in this life (Romans 2:1). God must—and will—punish us with death (hell) accordingly. Unless...

The Gospel is Good News. God sent his only Son, Jesus, to bear upon himself every ounce of punishment we deserve. God the Father crushed his Son, nailing him to the cross, killing him to provide us a way to escape our due for our many sins. When he raised him to life again on the third day, Christ conquered death and now God, in his infinite kindness, offers us life again instead of the death we deserve.

Freedom instead of punishment. Instead of a guilty conscience, a new start.

When we humble ourselves before God our Judge, confess our sins and accept by faith what his Son did for us, surrendering before him we can be saved. You and I move out from between the cross-hairs of God's just wrath. He embraces us at that point as his adopted son or daughter, purchased with the life of his Son. Reconciled and forgiven, we are free to enjoy our Creator like he originally intended. That is the love, grace and mercy of God.

There are only two possible places we can be in this world: Awaiting God's wrath or enjoying his love. Where are you? That is a bold question to ask but it is an absolutely necessary one. Nothing we do in life matters compared to knowing the answer.

Pleasant Places

I Have Seen, I Know, I Have Come Down

In rereading the story of Moses at the burning bush, look at what the Lord says to him in Exodus 3:7,8, "And the LORD said: ' I have surely seen...for I know...So I have come down to deliver.'"

God was aware of the bondage of his people under the cruel taskmasters of Egypt. Exodus 2:23 says, "Israel groaned because of the bondage, and they cried out; and their cry came to God because of [it]."

God is a rescuer, a deliverer. He willingly condescended to save his people from their helpless plight. And he didn't stop there. The message of Christianity is found in God's words above, "I have surely seen...for I know...So I have come down to deliver."

Every human being except the Lord Jesus himself has been held in hopeless bondage to sin. We, like Israel, serve a cruel taskmaster, the devil, and we do it "with rigor." Apart from Christ we only know pride, envy, lying, drunkenness, sexual immorality, drug addiction, gluttony, hatred in our hearts (murder), and on and on… Yet, God has surely seen the pain and destruction our sin has caused in our lives. He knows the wicked effects sin has brought upon humanity.

"So I have come down to deliver…"

Jesus Christ, the only God's only Son, left all his kingly glories in heaven, leaving aside the scepter, crown, and robe of royalty to be born like one of us, yet sinless, so that God himself would deliver us. Jesus died on the cross to pay the penalty for the sins of all he would ransom from the punishment they deserve.

There is a better way: God's Way.

Jesus said, "I am the Way" (John 14:6). God's compassion and mercy stopped at nothing—even killing his only Son—because he sees, he knows, and he wants to set us free. And he promises that just as he raised Jesus from the dead, we can be raised in new life in him.

God does not stop there. When he redeems sinners he puts them to a great and glorious work. Much like in the life of Moses in the next verses, 10 and 12, where God then says to Moses, "I will send you…" and "I will be with you," the Lord has sent his servants and is with them in the Great Commission:

> And Jesus came and said to them, "All authority in heaven and on earth has been given to me. 19 Go therefore and make disciples of all nations, baptizing them in the name of the Father and of the Son and of the Holy Spirit, 20 teaching them to observe all that I have commanded you. And behold, I am with you always, to the end of the age" (Matthew 28:18-20).

No other religion has its god saying such things as, "I have seen…I know…I came down to deliver." Not one. Call out to Christ. He is strong to rescue you like he rescued Israel. He will take your rigor and give you gladness in new, holy labor as you share what Jesus has done with others.

Pleasant Places

THE CHOICES WE MAKE WHEN NO ONE IS WATCHING

If you are a TV watcher, what TV shows do you watch when it is late at night and you can't sleep? If you are big on the internet, what sites do you visit when you are alone on the computer? If you are big on reading, what themes run through the books you curl up with? What do the articles and pictures in the magazines in your home promote? Is who you are when traveling alone, out of town on business, consistent with who you are at home?

The same probing questions can be asked about what you listen to in the car or how you react in it when you are running a few minutes late. The situations we find ourselves in when no one else is around to see the "real" us are many and varied.

What you most honestly think of God and his Son's instructions are manifested in your private choices. Remember what Jesus taught us:

> The lamp of the body is the eye. Therefore, when your eye is good, your whole body is full of light. But when your eye is bad, your body also is full of darkness. Therefore take heed that the light which is in you is not darkness. If then your whole body is full of light, having no part dark, the whole body will be full of light, as when the bright shining of a lamp gives you light (Luke 11:34-36).

If you have something you need to repent of in this area, I plead with you to do so. So much of what is readily available these days looks alluring. I understand. But I promise you, there is far more joy and pleasure to be found in a life that is pure and surrendered to Christ than in any sinful habit. In Christ there is always abundant mercy available to the one who repents. He can give you strength to resist like you never had before. The Lord can do the unthinkable!

Pleasant Places

CHRISTIANITY HAS FAILED?

Not long ago a friend posted on Facebook, "Today I saw two men holding a sign on the corner of a street that read: 'CHRISTIANITY HAS FAILED.'"

My friend didn't get to talk to the men. We have no idea what prompted them to stand there making their declaration. Whatever inspired them, they obviously felt strongly about their message. The problem of course, is that passion is not the same as truth. As someone once said, "You can be sincere and still be sincerely wrong." And these guys were sincerely wrong. Think about it:

Christianity has been around for 2,000 years and counting. It has millions of faithful adherents (and billions more who profess Christianity to one degree or another). In the name of its founder, Christianity has established hospitals, clinics, orphanages, schools, shelters, emergency services, and more, all around the world. And this has been going on non-stop for two millennia! ...And all of it was started by one itinerant peasant-preacher in some seemingly insignificant corner of the Roman Empire. Not even 35 years old, he was publicly executed as a criminal mainly because he claimed to be a King and he claimed to be God.

Yet these men say Christianity has failed. Hardly! The only failure I see is in their own conclusion. Of all the world figures throughout history, Jesus Christ is by far the most influential force for good, ever.

And he wants these two men to be saved.

Peter reminds us that God is, "not willing that any should perish but that all should reach repentance" (2 Peter 3:9). Even in the face of such blatant rejection, the Object of their scorn stands ready to pardon and offers them a place in his eternal kingdom. Pray for these two men that God would change their hearts and they would fall under the conviction of the Holy Spirit to repent and believe the Gospel. Wouldn't it be great to hear that one day these two men stood on the street holding a different sign: "JESUS SAVES."

Favorite Examples of God's Mercy

Scripture says over and over, "The Lord is good, and his mercy endures forever." Finding his mercy in creation, in life, and in the Scriptures is like finding sand on a beach—it's everywhere! There are so many other examples as we read through the Bible. These are some of my favorites. Whenever I read the Bible I can't help but be amazed at God's mercy.

Mercy in the Days of Noah
Scripture says that the Lord gave the people of Noah's day seven more days to repent before he would judge the earth through the Flood.

> Then the Lord saw that the wickedness of man was great in the earth, and that every intent of the thoughts of his heart was only evil continually. And the Lord was sorry that he had made man on the earth, and he was grieved in his heart. So the Lord said, "I will destroy man whom I have created from the face of the earth[...]"

> Then the Lord said to Noah, "Come into the ark [...] For after seven more days I will cause it to rain on the earth forty days and forty nights, and I will destroy from the face of the earth all living things that I have made " (Genesis 6:5-7a; 7:1,4).

Peter adds in 1 Peter 3:19 and 20, "…God's patience waited in the days of Noah, while the ark was being prepared..." Peter also calls Noah a "herald," or preacher "of righteousness." Noah built the ark. He also preached a message to the people warning them of judgment and calling for repentance and faith.

Mercy to Moses' Parents

This is one of my favorite examples of the nature of the Lord's kindness and generosity in all the Scriptures. Exodus chapter two tells the story of Moses' birth. At a time when the male Hebrew children were ordered to be slain, Moses' mother hid him as long as she could. At three months old she sent him down river in a little homemade basket, trusting God to take care of him. Pharaoh's daughter saw the basket in the reeds and had a Hebrew girl fetch it. Seeing a baby inside, she ordered the servant girl to find a Hebrew woman to help raise the child. And who did the girl go and get? Moses' mother! And God did even more—Pharaoh's daughter did not know the Hebrew woman was the baby's mother, but she paid the woman to raise the baby! That's right, God saved Moses and blessed his parents with an income and the joy of raising him. What a gift the Lord gave to Moses' parents.

Mercy in the Days of the Plagues in Egypt

When we think of the plagues, there are many ways we can think of God's mercy in them. First, the very fact that there were 10 plagues at all should astound us. The Lord could have moved straight to the death of every Egyptian firstborn and he would have been entirely justified; but he did not.

Second, the fifth plague was the destruction of livestock. In Exodus 9:5 Moses records that God told Pharaoh what he was going to do a full day in advance of doing it. "And the

Pleasant Places

Lord set a time, saying, "Tomorrow the Lord will do this thing in the land." Nevertheless, Pharaoh's will was unmoved. The next verse tells what happened next. "And the next day the Lord did this thing. All the livestock of the Egyptians died, but not one of the livestock of the people of Israel died."

Third, in the seventh plague, hail, God again gave a full day's notice of the destruction that was coming. He also warned the people of Egypt to protect every man and animal:

> Behold, tomorrow about this time I will cause very heavy hail to rain down, such as not been in Egypt since its founding until now. Therefore send now and gather your livestock and all that you have in the field, for the hail shall come down on every man and every animal which is found in the field and is not brought home; and they shall die" (Exodus 9:18,19).

MERCY REGARDING THE LIVESTOCK IN NINEVAH

The Lord often sent his prophets with messages to other cities and nations, calling on them to repent. Ninevah is one such city. Jonah (and later Nahum) was sent to preach a message of repentance to the people of Ninevah. Much to Jonah's annoyance, God cared enough to send him to warn the people in that "great city" to repent, even aware of the animals there.[8]

> And should I not pity Ninevah, that great city, in which are more than one hundred and twenty

---

[8] Thank you to Paul Washer for pointing this out in a sermon.

thousand persons who cannot discern between their right and their left—and much livestock? (Jonah 4:11).

Mercy Towards Us

The entire message of the Bible—of Christianity—culminates in his mercy in sending his Son to die in our place to save us—rebels who disobey time and time again! Romans 5:8 says, "God shows his love for us in that while we were still sinners, Christ died for us." When we see the lengths God went to save us from our sin and its necessary punishment, doesn't it make sense that our only fitting response to such kindness is to repent and serve him? This is why the Christian message makes sense. This is the logic of the Apostle Paul in his great statement in Romans 12:1. After spending the majority of his letter explaining humanity's guilt before God and God's great mercy through Christ now extended to people individually and to the nations, he says, "I appeal to you therefore, brothers, by the mercies of God, to present your bodies as a living sacrifice, holy and acceptable to God, which is your spiritual worship." There is none like God. No man-made religion or god has ever exhibited such patience and compassion as the Lord God.

Pleasant Places

EGYPT AFTER THE EXODUS

Imagine being an Egyptian after the Israelites left. The stubbornness of Pharaoh resulted in the whole nation being destroyed. The early and late crops you so depend on? Lost. Your valuable livestock? Dead by plagues. And, of course, the horror of every firstborn animal and human—all struck dead. Not a house in all Egypt escaped Yahweh's judgment.

And what of those initial days and weeks and months after the sudden and dramatic departure of the Israelites? The stench of death seemed as though it would never lift, made worse by the desert sun and heat. Mass burials hurriedly carried out across the land in place of proper funerals. Months of cleanup was needed. And everyone was asking, *What do we do with Goshen?*

An entire territory of Egypt was eerily *vacant*. Throughout the land where all the Israelites lived all that is left of them are their tens of thousands of empty dwellings. Well, not entirely empty. Every house likely had in it some furniture or fixtures left behind, belongings not worth taking in their sudden departure that fateful night.

As if the gruesome collection of dead first-born all over the country wasn't enough, or the wasteland of vacant Israelite homes, one final, chilling reminder remained.

We can't forget that when the Egyptians who survived the plagues would foray into the Israelites' former settlements there was something else they would see. On house after house, above door after door, lintel after lintel, were the haunting brush marks of blood. Once bright red, now dried and brown and permanently baked in. Streaks of lambs' blood. Over this house. Over that house. There. There. There and there. The marks that hastened death to the Egyptians were visible heralds of the Israelites' deliverance.

Surely these were Yahweh's special people.

Thirteen centuries later a Roman soldier stood beneath the blood-soaked cross on which a Jewish teacher was crucified. He heard that some even said he was their King, their "Messiah." As he stood guard nature itself reacted with darkness, thunder, and earthquakes. All he could mutter was,

Surely this was the Son of God.

JEHOVAH JIREH: THE LORD PROVIDES

In speaking of the Israelites' hurried exit from Egypt, Scripture says, "nor had they prepared provisions for themselves" (Ex 12:39). God could have told Israel to start making provisions the entire time of the plagues, and before; but he didn't. He knew they were leaving. He told them they were leaving. He knew they would need provisions for the nearly one million of them, plus animals. But he didn't say a word to them about it.

God was doing something. This was their first lesson that he was their chief Provision. God would supply all their needs. And sure enough, he did.

In every circumstance our provisions ultimately are given to us by the Lord. And yes, there may be times when we are caught by surprise by some tragedy or event that requires us to immediately get up and go like the Israelites. But the Lord was not surprised when it was time for Israel to depart and he won't be caught off-guard in our time of sudden, urgent travel, or at any other time. He will always be our chief Provision.

The Cloud, the Cross, and the Christ

Recorded for us in the story of the Exodus are the details of the pillar of cloud that covered the Israelites by day and the pillar of fire by night:

> And the Lord went before them by day in a pillar of cloud to lead the way, and by night in a pillar of fire to give them light, so as to go by day and night. He did not take away the pillar of cloud by day or the pillar of fire by night from before the people. (Ex 13:21, 22)

At the Red Sea, as Pharaoh's chariots chased after the Israelites.

> And the Angel of God, who went before the camp of Israel, moved and went behind them and stood behind them. So it came between the camp of the Egyptians and the camp of Israel. Thus it was a cloud and darkness to the one, and it gave light by night to the other (Ex 14:19,20).

Pharaoh's charioteers raced into darkness. They ran their horses headlong into chaos and judgment. The redeemed of the Lord traveled onward, under the light God provided, in the way he instructed them, to a place he determined—and eventually to a land "flowing with milk and honey."

Two Very Different Ends
One was headlong into obfuscation and the other upward toward revelation. One was to death and the other to life.

Pleasant Places

One sped onward in hardened disobedience while the other journeyed in God-given deliverance.

We see a similar divider in the New Testament, the cross of Christ. There are only two types of people in the world: those of think the cross is foolish and those who have come to know it as the power of God to salvation (1 Corinthians 1:18). As with the cloud, so with the cross. Just as the cloud divided between destruction and deliverance, so the does the cross.

Before Christ came into our lives, all we knew was darkness. If you do not know him today, the Scriptures say you are still in darkness. Apart from a life changed by the light of Christ, we have nothing to look forward to after death except a darkness worse than words. The cross of Christ brings light. Because of Christ we no longer have to remain in the darkness. Ephesians 5:14 puts it this way, "Awake, you who sleep. Arise from the dead, and Christ will give you light."

Do you know Christ's light today?

REFLECTIONS ON 1 PETER 1:1-5

> Peter, an apostle of Jesus Christ,
>
> To those who are elect exiles of the Dispersion in Pontus, Galatia, Cappadocia, Asia, and Bithynia, according to the foreknowledge of God the Father, in the sanctification of the Spirit, for obedience to Jesus Christ and for sprinkling with his blood:
>
> May grace and peace be multiplied to you.
>
> Blessed be the God and Father of our Lord Jesus Christ! According to his great mercy, he has caused us to be born again to a living hope through the resurrection of Jesus Christ from the dead, to an inheritance that is imperishable, undefiled, and unfading, kept in heaven for you, who by God's power are being guarded through faith for a salvation ready to be revealed in the last time (1 Peter 1:1-5).

As I read through this passage numerous things strike me. Consider:

v1 - Strangers/pilgrims - those who have no claim to the place they find themselves; passers-through. Does that describe me today? Are you comfortable in this world with its toys, games, diversions, anger, violence, sexuality, etc? Hopefully you and I live demonstrating this world is not our home.

v2 - "elect according to the foreknowledge of God" - People often debate the doctrine of election, despite it being clearly shown in Scripture. If election really meant "foreknowledge"

Pleasant Places

(i.e.: God fore-knew who would be saved—which he does anyway) than why would the Holy Spirit inspire Peter to write both words, "elect" and "foreknowledge"? God has clearly "elected" or chosen some.

v2 - "in sanctification of the Spirit" - It is the Holy Spirit who makes us more like Jesus.

v2 – "God the Father…the Spirit…Jesus Christ" – a reference to all three Persons of the Godhead

v2 - Why are we chosen? Why does God save us? The answer is surely not, *So we can live and do whatever we want.* Peter says it is, "for obedience." I once heard the statement, "Jesus does not own those whom he can't command."

v2 - "sprinkling of the blood of Jesus Christ" - Just as Moses sprinkled the people of Israel with the blood of animals to signify their being under covenant with God, we are sprinkled with the blood of Jesus himself into a much better and lasting covenant.

v3 - "according to his abundant mercy" - God the Father is abundantly merciful. When you are tempted to doubt God's mercy, by faith STOP. Remember his mercy. Recall examples of God's mercy from Scripture. How many can you name? How many from your own life?

v3 - Christians have now a "living hope" - a vibrant anticipation. But based on what? v3 - "through the resurrection of Jesus Christ from the dead." John agrees when he writes, "In him was life" (John 1:4).

v4 - Look at what is stored up for you: an inheritance incorruptible, undefiled, unfading, and reserved in heaven for… *you.*

v5 - That inheritance is not for everyone. If you do not know Christ you can write your name in there all you want, but it will do you no good. The promised inheritance is for those who are "kept" not by their own works but by "the power of God through faith for salvation"

Lots of people check their retirement accounts regularly to see how their investments are doing. The question that matters more is: Are you rich through God because of his mercy and faith to obedience, or are you, in actuality, bankrupt because you reject his goodness and kindness?

What Does It Mean to Say "God is Sovereign"?

The Bible declares repeatedly that God is sovereign. He is sovereign over the universe, this world, this world's systems and governments...everything. The Bible teaches that God is sovereign over every human being who has ever lived. He is sovereign over me and over you. But what does that really mean?

Thanks to Dr. Simon Kistemaker who, in his 1965 book *Calvinism: Its History, Principles and Perspectives*, includes this excellent explanation from Dutch statesman-theologian Abraham Kuyper:

> The word sovereign, says Kuyper, signifies that (1) I have made the object; (2) the object belongs to me; (3) I have laid down laws for this object; (4) the object as well as the elements out of which I have made the object are subject to me.

So, putting it all together: God has made you. You belong to him. He has laid down laws for you and me. Everything we are and everything we are made of are subject to our creator. These truths make unbelievers bristle. I know, I used to be there. And they make atheists furious. But they thrill the heart of everyone who has experienced the joy of surrender to the lordship of Christ.

Don't be a fool. Don't fight God. He is certainly sovereign. He is kind, good, loving, patient, and gracious. Humble yourself before your creator-owner and surrender willingly to his benevolent sovereignty before it is too late.

Anthony F. Russo

Salvation is not a cafeteria where you take what you want and leave the rest. You cannot take Christ as Saviour and refuse him as Lord and be saved.
 - Vance Havner

COSMIC JUSTICE? ARE YOU SURE YOU WANT THAT?

"There is cosmic justice in the universe." I was scanning the radio dial when I tuned to some station just in time to hear those words. The on-air personality, a woman whose name I did not catch, sounded rather "Aha!" about the whole thing, as though she was proving her point. I caught the remark just as she moved on to other things.

I turned the radio off and kept replaying her comment in my head, pop-quizzing myself as to how I would answer.

For one thing, her tone had a sly "us/them" quality about it as if to say, *We are the ones who are OK. Cosmic justice got the one(s) who really deserved it.* We can certainly sound humble about our self-righteousness, can't we?

I thought about her statement more. It wasn't just her tone; it was her whole statement that bothered me. Is there cosmic justice? Actually, yes, there is. The lady on the radio is right. There is cosmic justice. But it is not at all who (or what) she thinks it is. Suddenly my mind raced to the next logical conclusion...

LADY, YOU DON'T WANT COSMIC JUSTICE!

I said those words again aloud in the car almost hoping she could hear me. No, ma'am, that is the last thing you want. Your self-justifying self-righteousness is self-delusion. If you had any clue what the justice of the omnipotent One who made the cosmos is, you would be begging—*begging*—to avoid it.

The fact is, the Bible makes it clear that you and I by nature are the ones who are not "OK" before God. He is so holy he cannot tolerate, or even look upon, our innumerable offenses against him. His justice is fierce. It is ferocious. It is "cosmic justice" of the most terrifying, fearful sort and there is coming a Day when he will judge each and every one of us.

No, lady, you definitely don't want that kind of justice!

Maybe, reader, you don't believe in the God of the Bible. Maybe you hold to the idea that there is some personless karma in the universe. Maybe you are reading this book because you know me and you are curious what I would write. Or maybe a friend gave it to you. Whatever the case, I assure you it was no accident, and definitely not "karma." The God of the Bible led you here today.

You see, he is the Lord of cosmos. He spoke it all into being with just a word. And he graciously extends to us something infinitely better than cosmic justice: *cosmic mercy*. That mercy is freely available to us because his fierce justice—exactly what you and I deserve—was satisfied when he killed his only beloved Son on the cross 2,000 years ago. God the Father sent Jesus to die in your place as the propitiation (satisfaction) of God's own unwavering justice so that he could make his unfathomable grace and pardon available to undeserving sinners like you and me. It is available to all who turn from their sins, repent, and believe the Gospel (Good News) we have been discussing.

None of this is by nature what we want to hear, but it is what we need to hear. The last thing in the world any of us should want, if we really stop and think about it, is cosmic justice.

Pleasant Places

IS IT "CHRISTIAN" TO FEEL LIKE YOU HAVE NO WAY OUT?

Once when I was unsure what to do about a matter, a pastor I love and respect reassured me that, "God is not a God of confusion but of peace" (1 Corinthians 14:33). I took comfort in the reminder that the Lord loves his children; he does not play games with them. But, I admit that as I walked out of the pastor's office I was confused about confusion.

Look at what Paul says in 2 Corinthians 4:8, "We are hard-pressed on every side, yet not crushed; we are perplexed, but not in despair," (2 Corinthians 4:8). Did you ever wonder, if God is not the source of confusion, how could Paul freely admit that at times he was "perplexed"? Perplexed sounds like confusion. Hang on, the waters are about to get a little more muddy before they get clearer.

Strong's Exhaustive Concordance of the Bible defines the Greek word we translate as "perplexed" as to mean, "to have no way out; to be at a loss (mentally)." Amazing, right? The Apostle Paul actually wrote publicly about feeling as though at times he had no way out of situations. So, what can you and I learn from all of this?

That pastor was right to remind me that God is not, as the King James puts it, "the author of confusion." However, 1 Corinthians 14:33 has to do with orderly public worship, the place of speaking in tongues in worship, their interpretations, etc. "Confusion" here is used for a word that is talking about disorder, which is why Paul uses it as he does in the context of orderly worship. A synonym would be "chaos." God is not a chaotic God, nor does he want us to worship him in a frenzied, chaotic way (like what we often see on television or in some churches still today).

In English "confusion" and "perplexity" are largely synonymous, along with being "bewildered," "confounded," "befuddled," etc. The meanings are different in the original language. "Perplexed," as we saw, speaks to inward uncertainty. At times Paul was uncertain which way to go, but he was never confused about his calling.

God allows us to be perplexed at times. There is no sin in perplexity. Paul, as we have seen, was perplexed at times. The Psalms are God's gift to us partly because in them we read David's cries to the Lord in his times of perplexity. In our own seasons of perplexity we draw comfort from them for that reason. T.M. Anderson in his book, *Prayer Availeth Much* says

> There are times when our minds are sorely perplexed by the problems confronting us in this uncertain world. There are times when we cannot depend on our reasoning to find the answer to life's trials and tribulations.

God allows perplexity to sanctify us. Perplexity, like troubles, persecutions, sufferings, and a million other life experiences are used by the Lord to grow us in faith. An old hymn written in the early 5th century by Synesius of Cyrene, Bishop of Ptolemais says:

> *Lord Jesus, think on me,*
> *Nor let me go astray;*

Pleasant Places

Through darkness and perplexity
Point thou the heavenly way.[9]

Do not despair. I have saved this point until now. What did Paul say after he acknowledged his own perplexities? He said that, yes, he was perplexed, "but not in despair." Some translations say, "but not despondent." The world wrings its hands in anxiety and hopelessness—and rightfully so. They have no hope. There is a blessed difference for we who are born again by the Spirit of God. All who are in Christ have the promise that, "for those who love God all things work together for good, for those who are called according to his purpose" (Romans 8: 28). Cling to Jesus in seasons of uncertainty. He is the Way of salvation, and he is the Way out of perplexity. You are led by a Good Shepherd.

So how did my opening dilemma resolve? I don't know. I don't even remember what it was about. And isn't that fact a lesson in itself? Whatever it was, God took care of it.

---

[9] http://www.hymnary.org/text/lord_jesus_think_on_me_and_purge. Written by Synesius of Cyrene. Translated into English by Allen William Chatfield.

Anthony F. Russo

REFLECTIONS ON WORK

I used to think that work was a result of the Fall, that Adam was *cursed* to work for the rest of his life. I was wrong for several reasons. Adam worked prior to the Fall. Genesis 2:19-20 records for us that God put Adam and his God-given creativity to work to name the animals. The difference was that after the Fall everything, including the ground Adam worked, was cursed, forcing him to genuinely toil in his efforts.

In truth, God has blessed each of us with work. Humans have an innate desire to produce. The problem now is that since we are all children of Adam in this fallen world, whatever we set out to do is that much harder. All of us have struggled to learn something new. Growing up I tried to learn guitar several times. Then I switched to clarinet briefly. Then back to guitar. Then I gave up entirely. Maybe in high school you learned a different language, or physics. The worst part about working on a new skill is the uphill learning curve. Still, God is good, kind, and loving. Even in our toils the Lord loves us enough to redeem it for us. It is a common grace of God that hard work gets results and we find satisfaction in a job well done.

One way he does this by using the difficulties of work as a means of our sanctification. He uses those challenges to make us more like Jesus. The mundane elements of our jobs like those tasks or policies that annoy us, or the difficult coworker, and who our boss is are all—believe it or not—God's gifts. Yep, it's true. Did you think the people you work with and the experiences you have are only coincidences? Think again.

Pleasant Places

The Bible does not teach coincidence. Rather, it is God who orchestrates or allows everything. God put those people in your life and mine because he loves you and me. He wants us to learn what he means when he says to "do all things without grumbling or complaining" (Philippians 2:13-15 NKJV), to be "content with [our] wages" (Luke 3:13-15 NKJV), and to "do it heartily, as unto the Lord" (Colossians 3:23 NKJV)—all things that I, frankly, fail at daily.

One day the Lord will fully redeem us and this world. I believe in heaven we will do glorified work. Labor's curse will be lifted by the One who freed us and creation from its deadly grip. What is now cursed and toilsome will be blessed and perfected as it was meant to be in the beginning. Whatever challenge there may be in it then will only have a level of difficulty so that we can enjoy, in the purest sense, that God-given, satisfying feeling of accomplishment.

I can't buy you a car or a personal jet to fly over the stop-and-go traffic of your commute, but hopefully knowing how much God loves you and uses everything to make you more like Jesus each day makes those morning commutes a little easier.

Anthony F. Russo

The Curse is Gone, the Curse is Gone! Praise the Lord, the Curse is Gone!

What is your favorite Christmas song? There are many wonderful ones but my all-time favorite is "Joy to the World." For one thing, to play the opening notes on the piano you only have to walk your fingers down the scale to produce the familiar 8-note opening melody. Just being able to play it makes me happy. I can't play a real piano, but I am a Fisher-Price virtuoso.

The other reason I love this song is found in its third verse. When I started blogging in 2008 I had a feature that I did from time to time called Life in the Third Verse. Each devotional in the segment focused on the third verse of various hymns. Some of the richest beauty is tucked away in that musical hiding place. The third verse is like the church nursery worker or kitchen helper—they are the oft-forgotten, under-appreciated treasures of the church. Look with me at the third verse of Joy to the World:

> *No more let sins and sorrows grow,*
> *Nor thorns infest the ground;*
> *He comes to make His blessings flow*
> *Far as the curse is found,*
> *Far as the curse is found,*
> *Far as, far as, the curse is found.*

Isn't it beautiful? Isn't it glorious? Joy to the world, Jesus Christ has come! And, in coming he comes to vanquish sin and sin's curse over this world and over us. By Christ alone the cursed ground becomes blessed once more, as he meant

Pleasant Places

for it to be at creation. We were created to be special because we bear his holy image. Through the Fall we all became horribly marred by sin, subject to death and disease because of our disobedience through Adam. But by God's redeeming grace in Christ Jesus we have a Wonderful Savior now. The God-Man Jesus Christ, born of a virgin, comes in the likeness of his own creation to break the bonds of sin and sorrow that keep us captive. His willingness to die is our hope of forgiveness.

Through the cross and his empty tomb Christ has conquered death. Now he freely offers a share in his victory to all who come to him for life. His resurrected life is our hope of new and eternal life. And one Day sin will be done away with completely. What we only know in part now will be made perfect forever when he comes to rule and reign on his earth. Christ has come. Christ has won. The curse is gone. *Joy to the World!*

THAT DEFEATED TYRANT, DEATH

A professor in one of my earliest seminary classes introduced me to the writings of Athanasius, one of the Early Church Fathers. While only in his early 20s Athanasius wrote a treatise about Jesus coming to earth as a man called *On the Incarnation*[10]. Here is one of my favorite quotes from it. Look what he writes about Death:

> Death has become like a tyrant who has been completely conquered by the legitimate monarch; bound hand and foot the passers-by sneer at him, hitting him and abusing him, no longer afraid of his cruelty and rage, because of the King who has conquered him. So has death been conquered and branded for what it is by the Savior on the cross. It is bound hand and foot, all who are in Christ trample it as they pass and as witnesses to him deride it, scoffing and saying, "O Death, where is thy victory? O Grave, where is thy sting?"

> - Athanasius, *On the Incarnation*

No Christian need ever fear Death. Death is defeated. That old tyrant is defeated!

---

[10] You can read it for free here
http://www.spurgeon.org/~Philippians/history/ath-inc.htm

THE FOUR CRITERIA WE ALL USE TO DETERMINE WHAT WE BELIEVE

James Montgomery Boice once wrote, "Faith is believing in something or someone *on the basis of evidence* and then acting upon it" (James Montgomery Boice, *The Gospel of John: An Expositional Commentary*, Vol 1, John 1:1, p19, emphasis in the original). Anyone who says that Christians believe blindly is greatly mistaken. Granted, there may be some who do, but that is not the way God would have it. God gave us minds and expects us to use them. Actually, no matter what any of us believes, Christian or not, there are three main things we all must deal with to arrive at what we say we believe. What we believe about religion (or the lack of it) is really saying to the world that these are the ideas on which we are staking our lives now and eternity later.

THE WORTHINESS OF THE CLAIM

First, weigh the worthiness of the claim. Is the thing worth your time to even consider believing in? What will happen if you don't? What will happen if you ignore the matter entirely? In the case of the atheist, for example, in the short term ignoring the matter of God may not cause any immediate concerns. But, the most hardened skeptic has to rationally acknowledge the fact that even if there is only a .000001% chance that what they believe (and, by contrast, also what they reject) would affect their eternal afterlife, then they are obligated to give the matter some level of objective consideration.

THE CLAIM ITSELF

Second, be clear about the claim(s) itself. The claims of Christianity are, to the natural man, utterly absurd (1 Corinthians 1:18). We assert that 2,000 years ago a peasant, living in an insignificant corner of the Roman Empire, was God come to earth as a human being. Furthermore we believe that although he died a criminal's public death, he was completely innocent—that he never once sinned. We believe that this God-Man also came back to life on the third day after his execution. We assert that he was seen by many people over the next 40 days, and then ascended bodily into heaven. Christianity also claims he will return again at any moment to judge every person who will have ever lived—either to eternal reward or eternal damnation based upon their knowledge of, and acceptance or rejection of him as Lord. And he will thereafter rule the physical and spiritual universe forever.

Evaluate the Evidence

Third, evaluate the evidence of the claim. In the case of Christ and Christianity, such evidence includes the historical reliability of the Christian writings/Scripture, prophecy/fulfillment, the words and actions of Christ himself, the veracity of eyewitness testimony—and how many? Are they corroborating? What about the long-term life changes (if any) of true adherents? Don't get me wrong, historic and apologetic facts will never save anyone; but God can use them in the process of drawing men and women to the Scriptures, and ultimately to himself.

Decide

Fourth, decide. Once some amount of information has been carefully reviewed, make a decision. Can you say truly that you have taken reasonable time to honestly consider Christ?

Pleasant Places

How do you know the data you evaluated was accurate, and not hearsay? Did you give Christ an objective study? Pontius Pilate desperately tried to avoid making a decision about Jesus. His cowardice was his decision about Christ. In reality, when Jesus stood before him, Pilate was the one on trial, not Jesus. And so it is with us. Christ is not the one on trial. We are.

Perhaps you are not a Christian. Maybe you think you are a Christian because you grew up in a Christian home, or maybe you go to church. Let me speak candidly with you for a moment, as someone who has been there myself. Unless you have an ongoing relationship with Christ that began with an earnest repentance over your sin and continues in a life of ongoing love for him through obedience and charity, you very likely are not truly born again. That may offend you. Only you and God know for sure, but I would plead with you to ask the Holy Spirit to reveal the true nature of your relationship with him, and then accordingly on what he tells you.

Maybe you are reading this and you know you are not a Christian and have made the conscious decision to reject Christ. As I said in my introduction, I too once rejected God entirely. If you've read this far, hopefully you will at least agree that I have enough mental capacity to put ideas into words, then into sentences, then paragraphs. If I tell you, from one human being to another, that you owe it to yourself to explore fully the vast evidence for Christ and his claims, would you at least acknowledge that a reasonable, thinking person is appealing earnestly and respectfully to you through these pages?

Maybe you don't believe in Jesus Christ or the Bible. But you do believe in someone or something. John Calvin said the human heart is an idol factory. We can't help but worship something. What evidence has convinced you to place your faith in whatever person or ideas you espouse? Is that evidence strong enough that you are willing to stake eternity on it? Because right now that is what you are doing.

Which brings us back to Boice's comment at the beginning that faith is believing on someone or something based on the evidence and then following through—or as he says, "acting on it." There is no worldview we can hold that is as cohesive and credible as the Christian worldview. I implore you to weigh the worth of Christ, consider Christ, evaluate the evidence for Christ, and ultimately decide to worship Christ.

Spiritual Warfare

The notion of spiritual warfare gets a lot of bad publicity. There is a great deal of sensationalism attached to it thanks in part to Hollywood and (I think) Christian denominations and groups that over-emphasize this particular doctrine in their teachings. For some people everything is the result of spiritual warfare. Got a flat tire? *Spiritual warfare.* Fired from your job (even though it was your own fault you showed up late everyday for the last six months)? *Must be the enemy.* Sneezed? *You might be under attack.* I might be exaggerating a little with my examples, but not much. Many people really believe whatever keeps them from becoming rich or achieving their full "potential" is spiritual warfare. That is a gross misunderstanding of spiritual warfare, the nature of God, and our purpose in the world.

The arrows of the enemy are real, directed, and at times clearly visible. That is true. But they are more subtle than we tend to think. Satan is more about guerrilla warfare than straight-on attack. So how can Christians know what real spiritual warfare looks like?

Are you busy in some new spiritual venture? Have you launched a new Christian endeavor, particularly one that could have far-reaching impact in the lives of others to win them to Christ? The forces of the enemy are aware of it and are determined to thwart the success of it.

Have you recently experienced some spiritual "mountain top" experience with the Lord? Has he graciously shown himself in some exciting way in your life that has resulted in a deeper commitment to him? That would earn you a spot in the cross-hairs, I'd say.

Is life suddenly filled with quirky skirmishes and oddball stuff that is making you cranky? I don't mean your average occasional bad week where the kids are sick, or the car is acting up. I mean are you finding that in the course of a day you are tempted to wrath or impatience?

If you are striving to live a faithful, Christ-honoring life, avoiding the daily temptations and fighting sin as much as any Christian can, yet trials come so fast that they make you think, *What is going on?* or if you answered *yes* to the above examples, there may be something going on. Can I prove it? No, but if you pray about it the Lord will give you wisdom and discernment. So, what happens next?

For one thing…Pray. Spend time with the Lord and tell him everything that is going on. Don't fight it yourself; you are not strong enough. (See what Michael the archangel did in Jude 9.) You are a lowly sheep, albeit a sheep with battle gear on (Ephesians 6), but your Shepherd, the Lord Jesus, guides you with his staff and wields a rod (club) to ward off attackers. Run to him, abiding under his care and in his word.

Use the brain and spirit God gave you. Go with what God may be saying to you as you read your Bible. Simply becoming aware that something might be up is a great first step, and a biblical one. "Be sober [self-controlled], be vigilant; because your adversary the devil walks about like a roaring lion, seeking whom he may devour" (1 Peter 5:8). Peter says in the next verse (1 Peter 5:9) to "Resist him." But how?

Stay strong in the faith. As the old saying goes, the best defense is a strong offense. Peter continues by saying, "steadfast in the faith." So pray to be steadfast. And, while

Pleasant Places

you are at it, pray for your Christian brothers and sisters around the world to be steadfast too, as Peter adds at the end of the verse.

Praise the Lord. Nothing makes the enemy more angry and repulsed than sincere praise to the Lord. Break out those "psalms, hymns, and spiritual songs, making melody in your heart to the Lord" (Ephesians 5:19). You may be experiencing a funk, a malaise, a spiritual melancholy as part of the enemy's efforts, but remember the truths of the Gospel, the limitless grace and mercy that saves you, and praise by faith.

A fair question to ask is: *How long will it last?* Beats me. In a sense, it won't end until the Lord calls you home. But I can tell you that it cannot last one second beyond what the Lord permits; and he is with you every step of the way. Just keep doing all the above and pray every day (and with your spouse if you are married) or ask a close friend(s) to pray with or for you.

Finally, remember: Christ has won the victory. The devil is defeated. His days are numbered. I have already told you earlier in this book about my particular love of the third verse of hymns. Well, here is another example. Take some encouragement from the third verse of Martin Luther's famous hymn, "A Mighty Fortress Is Our God":

> *And though this world, with devils filled,*
> *should threaten to undo us,*
> *we will not fear, for God hath willed*
> *his truth to triumph through us*
> *The Prince of Darkness grim,*
> *we tremble not for him;*

his rage we can endure,
for lo, his doom is sure;
one little word shall fell him.

10 REASONS CHURCH MATTERS

Hopefully your God-given conscience nudges you every Sunday *You ought to be in church.* Maybe you answer, *Why should I?* I can think of at least 10 reasons for regular attendance at a healthy, Bible-teaching church.

1. Church is worship. It is the primary means of corporate worship, given to us by God.

2. The Bible teaches us to. "And let us...not forsak[e] the assembling of ourselves together, as is the manner of some" (Hebrews 10:24, 25).

3. Acts 2:47 says it was the Lord himself who brought people into the church. If he thought church was a good idea, shouldn't we?

4. God inspired the apostles to write to the churches. There are Paul's epistles to the various churches, John's Revelation, including Jesus' words to the seven churches in chapters two and three, and by extension the whole Bible is a gift to the Church. It seems clear: God is greatly interested in churches that honor him. In fact...

5. God gave pastors and teachers to the Church to strengthen believers in the faith (Ephesians 4:11, 12). How do they do that? Primarily through pointing us to Jesus as they preach and teach the Scriptures.

6. Other than within our own homes and families, the local church is the primary place for believers to develop and practice God-given gifts (1 Corinthians 12-14).

7. God's people will naturally want to be around God's people. It is the first place outside of the home to practice love, forgiveness, and care for others. It is a place of understanding. Being a Christian in a world that hates holiness, righteousness and the things of God is difficult. It causes soul weariness. The local church is a safe haven for where we can get refreshed and strengthened (Romans 12:9-13). The full verse of Hebrews 10:25 in Reason 1 says, "not forsaking the assembling of ourselves together, as is the manner of some, but exhorting one another, and so much the more as you see the Day [of Christ's return] approaching." Church is about community.

8. God commands us to submit to authorities (Romans 13:1-7). After the home, the church is the next best place to practice submitting to and serving others (Romans 12:10; Philippians 2:3-4). If the thought of submitting to a pastor/teacher puts in your mind a picture of slavish obedience, it shouldn't. That is not God's intent. If church leaders are acting outside of what Scripture teaches, the Holy Spirit will direct you, and you may well need to leave (a whole topic in itself, but see Ezekiel 34, for example). As you are called to submit to authority in a local fellowship, those over you face stricter judgment from God for the care they have of your soul (James 3:1). When both are fulfilling their roles as God designed it is a beautiful balance.

9. Church reminds us of the Gospel. Which is the most important part of the church service: The music, the reading of Scripture, or the sermon? The answer is all of them, equally. You know you are in a healthy church when everything in the worship service exalts Christ, pointing to the Gospel.

Pleasant Places

10. Church is where we celebrate The Lord's Supper together. Jesus himself gave us this fellowship meal, symbolic of both his death and return. Believers around the world have celebrated this meal for 2,000, some even underground, persecuted for the faith.

Sadly, a faithful, biblical church is becoming harder and harder to find. The quest to find a church home can be a tiring one. If you are naturally introverted, visiting churches and meeting new people can be uncomfortable. In all of this and more, God gives grace. If we are faithful to honor him the Holy Spirit will bless our desires and lead us to a place where the Scriptures are taught, unity exists, and Christ is exalted. And when he does, invite a friend!

8 Essentials in a Good Church

I have made a lot of bad church decisions in my life. They all mainly revolved around either jumping from church to church, or not knowing what to really look for.

Looking back, I can say without a doubt that church-hopping was bad for two main reasons: First, there were enough different teachings about baptism, end times, and other doctrinal differences that it all confused me badly. When God truly saved me in 2005, I had 20 years of all kinds of theology and Bible views in my head. After God broke me and started to rebuild me, part of that process was a lot of un-learning all of that so he could start with a clean slate. Doctrine is important. Doctrine and theology are not bad words. As Christians we should know what we believe. Jesus never scolded the scribes and Pharisees for having doctrine, but for having *wrong* doctrine, twisting sound doctrine to suit themselves, or being hypocrites about the right doctrines.

The second reason church-hopping was bad was simply a lack of accountability. Rather than me submitting to God's means of Christian community—the local church—I did not realize it, but I always saw myself as above it. I was critical, and thought I knew better how to do this-or-that. That was my attitude and it was not at all what God says our attitude should be. (See the previous essay, "10 Reasons Church Matters" for more thoughts on this.)

It is true that no church is perfect. Some are better than others, and, sadly, some ought to be avoided at all costs! But what do we look for? Here are eight essential characteristics to look for in a church. If you find these, you've found a church that likely desires to honor God above all else. This is not a complete list, but I believe it will help you evaluate a church beyond the first impressions of the music, the preacher, and the people.

ORTHODOX

I don't mean Eastern- or Russian-Orthodox. "Orthodoxy" comes from the Greek meaning "correct+belief." Look for a church that holds firmly to Christianity's 2,000 years of established, non-negotiable tenets of the faith, often summed up in historic Christian creeds and catechisms.

THE BIBLE

Look for a church that affirms the Bible is inspired by God, infallible, without error ("inerrant"), *and* sufficient, meaning it alone tells us everything we need to know about God and our relationship to him. God's word is to be taken literally, except where it is clearly expressing analogy, hyperbole, poetry, and a handful of other literary devices. A healthy church will *not* regard it as an ancient collection of myths, stories, and allegories. "Literal" means, well, literal—a literal Creation, flood, parting of the Red Sea, Jesus' miracles, and so on…

A local church should welcome any commonly reliable translation you bring. (In fact, they should be happy to see you bring a Bible. More on this below.) If the church members or leaders say you should only read such-and-such version that's a red flag. Some translations are better than others, but no church should prohibit you from reading whichever one you want. If a church affirms one translation is "inspired" or more preferred by God than another, leave.

Speaking of the Bible... *Got Bible?* Take a look around when you visit. Do people bring their Bibles? Do they look old and worn? (The Bibles, not the people.) Are passages in the Bible referred to often in the service? Is the sermon faithfully explaining a Bible passage? A church that loves God loves his word.

GOD
Does the church you are considering affirm the doctrine of the Trinity? The Bible is clear in its presentation God is three-in-one, Father, Son, and Holy Spirit, infinite, eternal, spirit, who are co-equals and distinct Persons yet One. Yes, this is a mystery, but it is clearly what the Bible teaches.

JESUS CHRIST
He is fully God, fully Man, God's only Son. Does the church affirm the virgin birth? A church that strives to be faithful to the Scriptures will affirm "substitutionary atonement," meaning that Jesus paid the penalty for sins instead of those he saves. And they will also affirm Jesus' bodily resurrection from the dead and promised second coming.

SALVATION
"Salvation is by faith alone, in Christ alone." There is no other way to be saved (such as doing good works, simply being a "good person," etc.). There are no other intercessors or mediators than the Lord Jesus (e.g.: no Mary, no saints, priests, prophets, popes). A good church believes Jesus' own words, "You must be born again" in John 3:3 and will affirm that the new birth in a person's life brings with it a changed life evidenced by an ever-maturing love for God and conformity to his word, and love towards others.

BAPTISM AND THE LORD'S SUPPER
It is essential that a church value and practice these ordinances according to the Scriptures.[11]

TEACHING
Are Jesus Christ and the Bible esteemed above everything else? How can you tell? For one thing, if church is the place we go to get spiritually fed, what is on the sermon "menu"? After God soundly saved me in 2005, I eventually left a church because God began to show me week after week that the sermons I was hearing were not lining up with what I was reading in my Bible. The sermons were like a steady diet of self-help, ego-boosting feel-good stuff with a few Bible verses thrown in for good measure. It was like eating a steady diet of only candy bars—sweet, yes, but not good for you.

Listen carefully to the sermons you hear. Is the preacher trying to pick at emotional scabs ("felt needs") to elicit some kind of response, or is he plainly declaring what the Bible says? Incidentally, this is where verse-by-verse, book-by-book "expository" preaching really shines—you get the whole Bible over time and the preacher is forced to cover more than only the topics he likes to talk about. The Bible should be the focus. The points of the message should come directly and clearly from the Bible passage being preached.

THE GOSPEL

---

[11] As a Baptist, I believe these are "ordinances," not "sacraments." Provided we agree on the major-level doctrines, I respect the doctrinal differences on these matters that others may hold.

The Gospel, the Good News that is the central message of the Christian faith, should be heard clearly and often from the pulpit. The world needs to hear that Jesus lived, was crucified, and is now alive, and so do we. Repentance and faith towards God should be common refrains. Daily reliance upon God through prayer and his word should be welcome, familiar friends in every service and activity in the church.

WORSHIP

I don't mean contemporary style vs. traditional, but the *focus* of worship. It should be on God, not people. The music, the lighting, the words—none of it should be staged to manipulate emotions. Sentimental feelings alone are not worship. Jesus said that those who worship God do so in spirit and in truth (John 4:23-24). Can music move us? Yes, and that can be a good thing. Music, by design, is a gift from God. But music can also be employed to produce cheap emotionalism. The musicians are there to lead in worshiping God, not to glorify themselves or prep the audience for the pastor's message. Look around and see if "All things be done decently and in order" (1 Corinthians 14:40).

FINAL THOUGHTS

Being part of a Bible-believing church is a blessing and affords many precious opportunities. Of course, no church is perfect. Check out IX Marks Ministries' "The 9 Marks of a Healthy Church"[12] and their helpful Church Search[13] tool. It lists churches aiming to be solid, Bible-teaching fellowships, incorporating the "9 Marks," they list as key criteria. From

---

[12] http://www.9marks.org/what-are-the-9marks
[13] http://www.9marks.org/churchsearch

Pleasant Places

my Baptist perspective, a terrific Baptist organization, Founders Ministries, also has a list of churches on its website As you search for a church, remember Proverbs 3:5-6, "Trust in the Lord with all your heart, lean not on your own understanding. In all your ways acknowledge him, and he shall direct your paths."[14].

---

[14] http://founders.org/misc/chlist

THE FUTILITY OF MAN-MADE RELIGION

In my first year of seminary Amy and I rented a townhouse north of Orlando, Florida. One day I was walking around subdivision when I saw two kids, a boy and a girl each about 7 or 8, trying to ride their push scooters ...on a bed of rocks. Not the brightest idea. As you can imagine, they had little success. No matter how hard they pushed and strained, their wheels were no match for the rocks underneath. I watched as they kept trying. You would think one would turn to the other and say, "This was a dumb idea; let's give it up." Nope. They kept right on struggling across that rock bed. When they finally gave up both kids seemed really surprised by how poorly the experiment went.

That, my friends, is every man-made religion. Think about it. Don't we do the same thing? Except for Christianity, every single religion on the planet is founded on the futility of trying to reach God by our own works, or denying his existence.

But, Christian, don't laugh too hard…you and I are often as guilty of the same folly.

It is also, dear saint, exactly what you and I try to do when we try to get God's favor by our own efforts. For a second I thought I was so much wiser than those little kids. Oh sure, when I was their age I tried dumb things like that, but I am older. I am smarter. *Oh really?* I heard myself say.

And how about when you feel like God isn't hearing your prayers so you try to pray "harder"?

Pleasant Places

…Or when you feel like you aren't a "good" Christian because you woke up late and only read ONE Bible chapter before rushing off to work?

…Or you know in your mind that God has forgiven you for your sin, but in your actions you double-down in your attempt work to earn God's forgiveness about some sin?

And in that moment, that boy and that girl who were decades younger than me, who had far less education, and may not have ever heard of Jesus in their little lives taught me more than I ever thought possible.

There is only one religion that rescues us from the impossible path of human effort: Christianity. God is gracious. He sent Jesus to make a better way: Himself. God now extends a means of pardon and forgiveness to all of us and "commands all men everywhere to repent," (Acts 17:30). God calls us to turn away from all forms of wickedness, including our vain man-made plodding to earn God's favor, and to believe in his Son Jesus Christ for salvation.

No Less Days

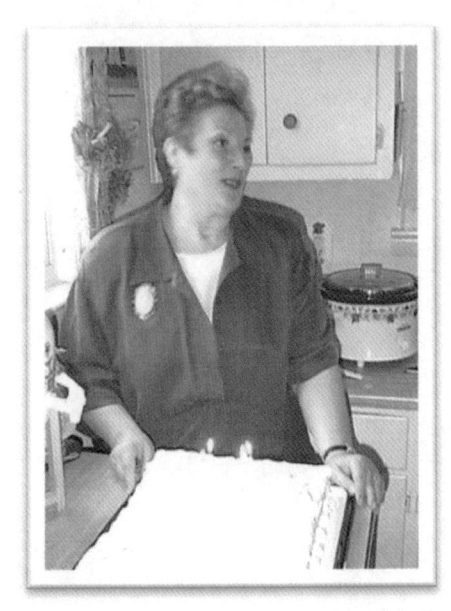

I originally posted this picture of my mom on my blog January 12, 2011. It was the 9th anniversary of her passing. Felicia Bauerle was only 59 when she died from metastic breast cancer. In the end, cancer was everywhere.

A week before she died, mom grabbed the cardboard tube from an empty paper towel roll and amazed us right there in her tiny kitchen with an impromptu show of her days as a twirler in the high school marching band. Rotating her wrist, she pretended to "twirl" the tube. First she held it high, then low; in the right hand, then passed to the left. Then, reaching down and passing it between her legs and up high again… All of us knew her routine had more comedy than grace, but that's what made it fun. And you know, for being tethered by a 50-foot tube of plastic that went from around her head, down, and across the floor, and into that constantly-whirring oxygen machine, she could still twirl. Her eyes were bright with vitality as she smiled with surprise and reminiscence. *Pretty good still, huh?* Better than *good*, Ma. Great.

Pleasant Places

The next memory I have of those days is my sister and I taking turns through the night administering the morphine hospice gave us. A couple drops from an eye dropper to in-between mom's dry, chapped lips should not have been so difficult. We were afraid we would either break her or drown her. Every now and then between doses she would moan. Short moans, like someone talking in their sleep. We would jump up and see what we could do for her. *Do you need water? Do you need to go to the bathroom? Are you cold?* No answer; she was back to sleep. This went on for a couple days. Then Saturday morning came.

Most of us were gathered around her as she sat upright on her sofa. She stayed there all the time, even sleeping sitting up once it got to be too hard to breathe while lying down. The oxygen machine had this weird way it mimicked her faint breathing, the fan sounding slightly different as if it, too, was breathing in and out. And then it didn't. That's when I noticed it. The rhythmic cadence I grew familiar with was now a person-less droning. It all happened in a few seconds. We all looked at each other and then at mom. Her chest wasn't rising. Her eyes had been shut for a couple days but they were open, wide and clear, and staring out the small window in her living room. We waited a minute, but we knew. After we called hospice I went into her bedroom where the oxygen machine was.

The sudden silence startled me. I did not realize how accustomed to its noise I had become. This may sound strange but I took great joy in turning off the oxygen. I knew mom's faith. I knew that she did not lose her battle with cancer. Because of her faith in Jesus Christ, she won.

After she passed and her small estate was settled, each of us grown children inherited money and divided her few possessions. We each took the photographs and furniture we wanted. We divided all the usual mementos and donated whatever was left to charity. We all agreed my brother should have her Bible. I asked for the next best thing: her dusty pink dollar store reading glasses. I know it doesn't sound like much but whenever I would visit I would see them on her face. They're tucked away in a box in my basement. They've moved with me from place to place over the years. Why do I keep a cheap pair of "cheaters" as she called them? Because I still smile remembering what she looked at the kitchen table or in the living room as she sat reading her Bible.

Fast-forward to today. You already know of my secret stash of treasures hidden in plain sight in the third verse of many hymns. "Amazing Grace," is a song about how Jesus Christ changes lives, even a "wretch" like slave trader John Newton. Jesus Christ changed my mother's life. With apologies to John Newton, in his hymn, "Amazing Grace," I've learned to treasure the fifth verse—the one he did not originally write. The verse was added later by John P. Rees. It goes,

> *When we've been there 10,000 years,*
> *Bright shining as the sun,*
> *We've no less days to sing God's praise,*
> *Then when we first begun*

I always think of my mom in this verse. As I edit this essay it is a few days before 2014 and now the 12th anniversary of her passing. There is no time in Heaven, but humanly speaking in another 9,988 years she will still have *no less days* to sing God's praise. I miss her very much. We did not get along for many years, but God gave grace and restored our relationship

Pleasant Places

in the last two years we had. There are so many things that have happened in my life since that I wish I could share with her. Some of them she is better off not knowing. Most of all, I wish she could have met Amy. She would love Amy. Although I miss her, I am happy mom is with Jesus. Because of his Amazing Grace and the hope of the power of his resurrection, I look forward to being there in Heaven with her.

Maybe you miss a loved one who knew Jesus and is gone now. You and I grieve together. Our joy for that person is tinged with earthly sorrow. The comfort in John Rees' words is for you, too. Jesus wept at the tomb of his friend, Lazarus (John 11:35). He is still our friend in our mourning on this side of eternity. But he reminded Mary and Martha he was the resurrection and the life. All who were in Christ on earth are in Christ forever. That is "Amazing Grace." That is the Gospel. And 10,000 years from now, that will still be our song.

Anthony F. Russo

What Does Your Facebook Profile Say About Your Faith?

Have you ever thought about that? I hope you have. I have. A lot of Christians, it seems to me, have not. It is common to look at a Christian's profile page and see under Political Views: Conservative, and under Religious Views: Christian. Especially here in America, Christians tend to be outspoken about those views.

Unfortunately, many also say and share things better left unsaid.

A lot of people post Bible verses as their *FB* status. I do sometimes. Nothing wrong there, nor do I think that should be the only thing we post. However, I have seen professing Christians post statuses that are so worldly I get confused as to who posted them—*Whoa, a Christian posted that?* If I have to wonder, and I'm Christian, what message are we sending to non-Christians?

I've been on Facebook since 2008, first as a way to keep in touch with college-age men and women we met on an evangelism mission trip. Since then I've been saddened on more than one occasion when I see Christians post crude jokes, petty grumblings about all kinds of things, comments with the abbreviation "lmao"[15], and—my personal pet-peeve—sad song lyrics or vague, cryptic little status updates used as emotive (and sometimes bizarre) cries for attention. I have seen them all ...from Christians.

---

[15] If you don't know what this means, be glad.

Pleasant Places

Going back to the Profile page, there is a lot to be learned about someone by what they list as their Activities and Interests. Again, in the case of Christians, I have been left somewhere between confused and saddened at times. I've seen inappropriate movies and TV shows "Liked" as favorites, singers and bands who haven't sung a clean song lyric ever listed as favorite artists, and so on. We have just as much obligation to be careful on Facebook and social media so as not to cause others to stumble as we do in real life. I am not saying we need to list Isaac Watts or Fanny Crosby as our favorite artists, but the point is: Where is our holiness? When our lost friends (and remember, without Christ they are truly lost) read our profiles and posts do they perceive us as different at all?

Try this: Read over your profile page with the fine-toothed comb of a cynical, watching world. Go back over your past status updates for the last month or year. Does your Facebook witness send a confusing message to your unsaved friends? Can you reconcile in your mind how your unsaved friends perceive that your profile says you love both a bunch of R-rated movies *and* Jesus? Or the Bible *and* many of the same things the world also loves? Look at your witness on Facebook for inconsistencies. Pray for the Lord to show you any idols. Then smash them quickly.

Look at what James writes:

> From the same mouth come blessing and cursing. My brothers, these things ought not to be so. Does a spring pour forth from the same opening both fresh and salt water? Can a fig tree, my brothers, bear

> olives, or a grapevine produce figs? Neither can a salt pond yield fresh water (James 3:10-12).

Dear brothers and sisters in Christ, you and I are ambassadors of the Most High God to this world. The inappropriate, ungodly things Christians post their Facebook profiles and updates confuse non-Christians and frankly, they confuse me. James' words are worth repeating, "these things ought not to be so."

The Bible doesn't speak directly about Facebook or social media, obviously. But it does speak a lot about a Christian's character, conduct, and testimony. What it says applies to our lives both in the real world and online. Facebook asks *What's on your mind?* And what you write for the world to see exposes your heart. And as far as that goes, Jesus said it best:

> The good person out of the good treasure of his heart produces good, and the evil person out of his evil treasure produces evil, for out of the abundance of the heart his mouth speaks (Luke 6:45).

So how can we avoid this and be more careful about our online witness? Consider using Paul's words to the Philippians as the "rule of heart'" for how you interact online and what you post:

> Finally, brothers, whatever is true, whatever is honorable, whatever is just, whatever is pure, whatever is lovely, whatever is commendable, if there is any excellence, if there is anything worthy of praise, think about these things (Philippians 4:8).

I'll give James the final word on all of this:

Pleasant Places

Who is wise and understanding among you? By his good conduct let him show his works in the meekness of wisdom (James 3:13).

Anthony F. Russo

How to Go to Heaven — In Five Words

…his mother said to the servants, "Do whatever he tells you" (John 2:5).

The context here is Mary, Jesus' mother, speaking the servants at the wedding in Cana. She just escalated the problem of no more wine to Jesus to resolve. She turns from the Lord and tells the servants plainly, "Do whatever he tells you." Sure enough, Jesus instructs them to fill the large earthen water pots nearby with water, dip a ladle in and bring it to the master of the feast. Jesus' first miracle in his earthly ministry occurs: water becomes wine.

Maybe it is my New Jersey upbringing, but I can't help but read a strength and spunk in Mary's words. Yes, she was godly and humble, and from her youth had a wisdom about her, but that was thirty years ago in the narrative. She is all that and more by now. I see in her words to Jesus and the servants a strong, confident woman who knows how to take charge, yet without being domineering. With wisdom and poise she quietly manages the wedding host's embarrassing situation by escalating the matter to Jesus, the One who could fix it, and instructing the servants in what to do next. What an example of godly leadership.

There is more here for us. There is an irony that it is Mary whom Scripture records giving these instructions. Her instructions point to Jesus. They magnify Jesus. They direct others not to look at her for the solution, but to him. In fact, years before, when Mary first found out the Lord had chosen her to bear the Son of God, she sang a song of praise to the

Pleasant Places

Lord, "and my spirit rejoices in God my Savior" (Luke 1:47). Mary acknowledged her need of a Savior. Mary, it has been noted, knew then that although she was a godly young woman, she was not perfect. She too needed to be saved from her sins. How ironic is it, then, that millions around the world revere—and even worship—this one who always directed the glory and the attention to the Lord? She would be so disappointed at their misguided veneration.

Mary's words are more than orders to servants to fix a temporal problem at a party. They lead us to eternal life. Eternal life is found only in Jesus. Only through his words can we find eternal life.

How do we go to heaven?

Do whatever he tells you.

In God's Bankruptcy Court

When it comes to filing personal bankruptcy in the United States, there are two main ways to file. One is Chapter 7, you prove you are helpless to pay your debts and petition the judge to forgive all your debts, and thus wipe your credit slate completely clean. The other, Chapter 13, is for when you negotiate with your creditors in court to pay back much less than what you really owe. Chapter 7 discharges the debt completely; Chapter 13 is a partial repayment plan.

Coming to God is a little like coming before the judge to petition for personal bankruptcy. However, the debt is far greater, and God—who is both your Creditor and your Judge—is under no obligation to forgive your massive debt of sin against him. In God's bankruptcy court, there is only one way to file.

With God, there is no such thing as filing Chapter 13. There is no trifling with any ridiculous idea that somehow, someway you can work to pay off some of your debt of sin through being a better person or trying harder. You never can and you never will. And he would never agree to such a lesser debt anyway. God must uphold justice. He is the one to whom you and I are ultimately hopelessly indebted and he has every right in the universe to demand full payment.

Of course, he knows you and I cannot pay it. Nor does he want us to. God in his mercy devised a much better plan. His plan is so astonishing that it is actually even scandalous. In fact, "scandal" is the very word used in the Bible to figuratively describe it. God satisfies what is due him and also provides a legitimate way for you and me to petition for full bankruptcy and plead for mercy and forgiveness of our debt.

Pleasant Places

But we must do it on *his* terms. Only a full and complete admission of our utter spiritual insolvency, believing in faith that Jesus alone paid our debt of sin on the cross will effect God's mercy and forgiveness.

The Gospel is this: If we come to God admitting our hopeless debt of righteousness towards him, acknowledging that we are destitute and bankrupted by sin, and if we call upon Christ alone to come to our aid, then God our Judge becomes God our Savior; and we are made free to leave his courtroom richer than we could ever imagine.

Anthony F. Russo

HOW WOULD YOU INTRODUCE YOURSELF?

(This is one of the first devotionals I ever wrote. - AR)

If you had to introduce yourself—just on paper—to someone who doesn't know you, how would you start? Oh, and you can't give your name, or tell what you look like or how old you are, or what gender you are, or where you live, or… In fact, let's say the only introduction you have is to tell the reader about an accomplishment of yours—and not even one of your best ones. Lastly, try doing all of this using about 10 words. Here is the space for your 10 words:

____ ____ ____ ____ ____ ____ ____ ____ ____ ____ .

How did you do? Pretty tough assignment, huh?

What is amazing is that God introduces himself to you and me in exactly that way. Genesis means "beginning." Look at Genesis 1:1, the very beginning of the Bible:

"IN THE BEGINNING GOD CREATED THE HEAVENS AND THE EARTH."

Let's look at this more closely.

IN THE BEGINNING, GOD

God existed before the beginning. God has always existed. Just as you wouldn't attempt to prove *your* existence to someone, neither does God. And what does the word "God" mean? Genesis was written in Hebrew. The Hebrew word for God here signifies supremacy and strength. In four words we learn God that is ageless and ultimate strength, and not *a*

Pleasant Places

god, but *the* Supreme Being. But hold on, he didn't stop there.

CREATED THE HEAVENS AND THE EARTH
God is creative, detailed, structured, completely comfortable working in the grand scale of nebula and galaxies as well as the invisible scale of molecules and atoms.

God tells us quite a bit about himself in 10 words. The more one reads the Bible, the more one learns about him. In the opening sentence we learn he is ageless, supreme, logical, orderly, creative and caring enough to make this world environmentally hospitable to human habitation, and beautiful and all for us to enjoy.

Whether you are a Christian reading the Bible for inspiration or a skeptic looking for holes, ask God to show himself to you as you read it. You'll undoubtedly discover that the first book of the Bible, Genesis, really is only *the beginning*.

Suffering Weighed in the Scales

Christians sometimes share Scripture verses with each another like others share stock tips. One time a Christian brother called out to me as he was leaving, "Hey, check out Romans 5:1-5!" Here it is:

> Therefore, since we have been justified by faith, we have peace with God through our Lord Jesus Christ. Through him we have also obtained access by faith into this grace in which we stand, and we rejoice in hope of the glory of God. Not only that, but we rejoice in our sufferings, knowing that suffering produces endurance, and endurance produces character, and character produces hope, and hope does not put us to shame, because God's love has been poured into our hearts through the Holy Spirit who has been given to us.

What caught my eye were the nouns that are ascribed to believers as present possessions: faith, peace, access, grace, joy ("we rejoice"), hope, endurance, and character. Imagine those on one side of a pair of scales.

Now look at what counter-balances them: Sufferings.

The scales are not tipped out of balance. Rather, they are perfectly balanced for Christian maturity. Nobody wants suffering. However, without it our lives in Christ would be out of balance. Those seasons draw us into the joy of knowing the Lord more deeply precisely because they cause us to lean on him more. That is not to say that our suffering

Pleasant Places

is what causes us to be justified or to have peace with God. Not at all. Paul begins this chapter with the word, "Therefore." What he is hearkening back to is in the last verse of Chapter 4, "Jesus our Lord, who was delivered up for our trespasses and raised for our justification." Everything that gives us peace with God is because of *Jesus'* suffering in our place, for our sin.

The scale is balanced because our sufferings are in our lives with our Father's full knowledge. Whatever discouragements, sadness, illness, difficulties, or persecutions we face—he knows them all. It is his good design that they produce in endurance, character, and hope. They cause us to call on Jesus more, even if that means we call on him through tears.

Creation in Six Literal, 24-Hour Days?

One of the first objections when someone challenges the Bible is, "So you really believe God created everything in six 24-hour days?" There is simple answer to that question.

The folks at Answers In Genesis[16] have done a wonderful job with this challenge. In short: Before sin entered the world there was no death. No creature, down to the lowest organism, could have yet died. So it is impossible that creation could have occurred over millions of years. This same fact also disproves the theory of evolution.

Secondly, God is God. The true miracle of creation is not that God created everything in six 24-hour days—it is that he chose to take so long. He is the Lord of everything. He could have easily created it all in six seconds. And even that would be a long time for the One who only spoke a word to bring it all into being out of nothing.

So, *Creation in six literal, 24-hour days?*

Yes, of course!

---

[16] http://www.answersingenesis.org/creation/v18/i1/sixdays.asp

THE BIBLE: AUTHORITY FOR EVERYTHING IT TOUCHES

Matthew Fountaine Maury (1806-1873) is known as the Father of Oceanography. Using Psalm 8:8 as his guide ("the birds of the heavens, and the fish of the sea, whatever passes along the paths of the seas") he was determined to learn what the paths of the seas were. And he did. Maury discovered what we today know as ocean currents. Even the Wikipedia article about him acknowledges his total reliance up on Scriptures for his endeavors, "Maury lived by the Scriptures; he fully and unconditionally believed in what the Holy Scriptures stated; he hardly ever spoke or wrote without the inclusion of scriptural references; he prayed every day."[17]

Maury's daughter, in her 1888 book about her famous father, records his words:

> I have been blamed by men of science, both in this country and in England, for quoting the Bible in confirmation of the doctrines of physical geography. The Bible, they say, was not written for scientific purposes, and is therefore of no authority in matters of science. I beg pardon! The Bible is authority for everything it touches...The Bible is true and science is true, and therefore each, if truly read, but proves the truth of the other.[18]

---

[17] http://en.wikipedia.org/wiki/Matthew_Maury as of 1/11/2014
[18] Diana Fontaine Maury Corbin, *A Life of Matthew Fontaine Maury*

Maury was a wise man. The Bible is not a science book, per se, but where it does reference scientific things, it is trustworthy. The same holds true for history, archeology, and of course, theology. This is often argued as being an error of circular logic; we say the Bible is true because the Bible says it is true. If we were talking about any other book it would be an error of circular logic, however, it is not precisely because it is the Bible. Do Christians need to defend this exception? No.

Certainly Christians can show proofs for the validity and authority of the Scriptures. When an opportunity presents itself with someone who is genuinely curious, we should walk with the inquirer through the facts. One of the greatest misconceptions I hear from Bible objectors is that it is a book that was written by a man. No, it was actually written by over forty different authors. Another objection raised is that men deviously selected what books made it into the Bible to control other people. Nonsense! Learned men selected the books which made it into the final canon based on careful criteria such as:

- A particular book's overall agreement with other books (unity)
- Was it referenced by Jesus or the apostles?
- Was it quoted and acknowledged as Scripture by the Early Church Fathers?
- Was the book historically accurate?
- Did the book have a high quality of internal consistency?

I have heard preachers give the example of how, when a police officer pulls over a speeder, the officer does not have

Pleasant Places

to first argue the validity of the law that was broken with the offender. "Ma'am, before I give you this ticket, you're right, I need to prove to you that there really is this law about the speed limit; it is a valid law; explain why you are required to obey it, and prove that you broke it." Of course not. In the same way, the Bible doesn't need us to prove its authority over everything, including over the lives of every human being. As Matthew Maury would say, "I beg pardon! The Bible is the authority for everything it touches!"

Anthony F. Russo

WE CAN TRUST THE BIBLE, PART I

For those of us born after John F. Kennedy, how do we really know he existed? In the movie *Forrest Gump*, by inserting Tom Hanks' Forrest Gump character into famous historical scenes Hollywood proved with humor and special effects that you can't trust what you see. It looked like Tom Hanks/Forrest Gump was everywhere in recent history. What if you never saw footage of President Kennedy, but only some relic from the past tied to him? It would take a great deal more faith to believe President Kennedy existed by seeing a desk he supposedly sat at or a pen he allegedly used. Well, if you swear by science as your supreme source for all things true you are in for a big disappointment. Science and its scientific method cannot reproduce JFK in order to prove he once existed.

So, again, I ask: *How do we really know JFK existed?*

Before you quit reading and write me off as a conspiracy nut, I do believe he existed. I believe because of the overwhelming evidence of eyewitness accounts, historical documents, and facts recorded by qualified historians. Holocaust deniers, on the other hand, refuse to believe the Holocaust happened because they refuse to believe the evidence. They utterly refuse to believe the mountain of verifiable evidential support for the fact of the Holocaust. Rejecting credible historians, such people favor "historians" of the lowest order instead. The point is this: Eyewitness testimony and evidence play a big part in what we determine is true.

What about the Bible? There is no reason whatsoever we should not subject the Bible to the utmost scrutiny if we are

Pleasant Places

to believe it. Are you surprised I would say that? Did you think I would argue we ought to take it on "blind" faith? What kinds of scrutiny? Well, how about:

- Internal evidence (What does it say about itself?)
- External evidence (What evidence outside of the Bible gives it credibility?)
- Historical accuracy (Does it reliably provide names, places, dates, cities, events, etc?)
- Authorial credibility (Were the writers like those "historians" of the lowest order, or not?)
- Textual fidelity (This answers the familiar question, "Hasn't the Bible been changed over these thousands of years?")
- Prophecy–yes, prophecy. (If it claims something would happen, did it?)

Many New Testament authors were eyewitnesses of Jesus. You can't get closer to the source than that. Peter was an eyewitness and wrote two books of the New Testament, and he is acknowledged as the primary source for Mark's Gospel account. Here is what Peter says of his own credentials:

"I who am…a witness of the sufferings of Christ…" (1 Peter 5:1)

And:

"For we did not follow cunningly devised fables when we made known to you the power and coming of our Lord Jesus Christ, but were eyewitnesses of his majesty…we were with him on the holy mountain [of transfiguration]" (2 Peter 1:16,18)

Historically, Peter is believed to have been crucified upside-down for his testimony about Jesus. If he was perpetuating "cunningly devised fables" it is implausible to think he would subject himself to the horrors of such torture for a lie. (And the same can be said of all of the other Apostles, most of whom were also martyred; John lived out his days in exile.)

I have not even begun to list all of the evidence in support for both the Old and New Testaments. The Bible can most certainly be trusted. It is no made-up story like something out of Hollywood. In fact, if someone tries to tell you the Bible can't be trusted...*Run, Forrest, Run!*

WE CAN TRUST THE BIBLE, PART II

Eyewitnesses are an important part of most any court case. Multiple highly credible eyewitnesses are ideal, the kind who will stand up to the scrutiny of the most aggressive cross-examinations.

The Bible commands us to believe and obey it, warning us that our eternal souls are in peril if we ignore what it teaches. Well, if anyone handed me a book and said that to me I'd think they were crazy. So two immediate questions, then, are: Is the Bible just a regular book? And, what authority does it have to make such demands upon me, and on all of us?

In my last essay I talked about Peter's eyewitness credentials. This time let's consider the Apostle John's eyewitness statements:

EXHIBIT A: JOHN 1:14

> And the Word [Jesus] became flesh and dwelt among us, and we beheld his glory, the glory of as of the only begotten of the Father, full of grace and truth (John 1:14).

EXHIBIT B: JOHN 21:24-25

> This is the disciple who testifies of these things, and wrote these things; and we know that his testimony is true. And there are also many other things that Jesus did, which if they were written one by one, I suppose that even the world itself could not contain the books that would be written (John 21:24, 25).

EXHIBIT C: 1 JOHN 1:1-5

> That which was from the beginning, which we have heard, which we have seen with our eyes, which we have looked upon, and our hands have handled, concerning the word of life— the life was manifested, and we have seen, and bear witness, and declare to you that eternal life which was with the Father and was manifested to us— that which we have seen and heard we declare to you, that you also may have fellowship with us; and truly our fellowship is with the Father and with his Son Jesus Christ. And these things we write to you that your joy may be full. This is the message which we have heard from him and declare to you, that God is light and in him is no darkness at all. (1 John 1:1-5).

EXHIBIT D: REVELATION 1:1-2

Lastly, while living in exile for the faith which he held to, and about age 80, John writes:

> The Revelation of Jesus Christ, which God gave him to show his servants—things which must shortly take place. And he sent and signified it by his angel to his servant John, who bore witness to the word of God, and to the testimony of Jesus Christ, to all things that he saw (Revelation 1:1-2).

CONCLUSION

So, here is an eyewitness who lived almost into the second century, and for at least 50 years held unwaveringly to all that he saw in Jesus and received from him. John would be any lawyer's ideal eyewitness. Furthermore, his testimony has withstood 2,000 years of critical cross-examination. Peter and John are just two examples of superb eyewitness testimony corroborating the Person of Jesus and the validity of the Bible. Can the Bible be trusted? Absolutely.

Case Closed.

Anthony F. Russo

MORE FROM ATHANASIUS

Amazingly, some estimate Athanasius to only have been in his 20's when he wrote *Incarnation*. It is a great book to buy for someone who is investigating Christianity. An Early Church Father, Athanasius (c.297-373) wrote *On the Incarnation* to defend against heresies of his day that denied Jesus was fully God and fully Man and fully incarnate.

Athanasius writes with surgeon-like precision. He lays out his arguments clearly and simply. Every sentence is packed with insights for take-away contemplation, and the paragraphs (sections) flow evenly to present the reader with remarkably strong arguments adorned with logic and love. Consider a few quotes:

OF HIS LOVE AND SUBSTITUTIONARY DEATH

> Thus, taking a body like our own, because all our bodies were liable to the corruption of death, He surrendered his body to death instead of all, and offered it to the Father. This He did out of sheer love for us (p34).

ON JESUS BEING PHYSICALLY PRESENT AND ALSO GOD

> From such ordinary acts as being born and taking food, He was recognized as being actually present in the body; but by the extraordinary acts which He did through the body He proved Himself to be the Son of God (p46).

ON WHY JESUS HAD TO DIE PUBLICLY

> If He had died quietly in His bed like other men it would have looked as if He did so in accordance with His nature, and as though He was indeed no more than other men. But because He was Himself Word and Life and Power His body was made strong, and because the death had to be accomplished, He took the occasion of perfecting His sacrifice not from Himself, but from others. How could He fall sick, Who had healed others? (p51).

On The Multitude of Christ's Accomplishments

> In short, such and so many are the Savior's achievements that follow from His Incarnation, that to try to number them is like gazing at the open sea and trying to count the waves (p93).

Don't let the loftiness of the subject dissuade you, Athanasius is easy and enjoyable to read. Your faith will be enriched if you take time to read his short but important work.

But Can They Name Them?

Back in 2010 FoxNews had an article about scientists discovering 200 sextillion more stars in the universe.[19] How many is that? Well, depending on where you live, it is either 200 followed by 21 zeroes (in the United States and Canada) or, if you live in Britain, France, or Germany it is 200 followed by 36 zeroes. One thing is for certain: It is a lot. Let's put it this way, in the United States, our national debt at the time of this writing is somewhere around 17 trillion—that is "only" 17 with 12 zeroes after it, not 21.

It is a gift from God to have the technology that enables scientists to see that far into space. The photo that ran with the article displayed a beautiful colored and cluttered collage of galaxies, tilted and brilliant against a backdrop of the total blackness of deep space. And even that didn't began to show the full beauty of the discovery.

But now let's open the Bible and filter what we read in the news and see on TV through what the Scriptures say. Psalm 147 verse 4 says, "he determines the number of the stars; he gives to all of them their names."

Did you catch that?

The Lord not only determines the number of stars, he names each and every one of them. The prophet Isaiah adds:

---

[19] http://www.foxnews.com/scitech/2010/12/01/scientists-sextillion-stars/

Pleasant Places

> Who has measured the waters in the hollow of his hand and marked off the heavens with a span, enclosed the dust of the earth in a measure and weighed the mountains in scales and the hills in a balance? (Isaiah 40:12).

Of course, the answer to his rhetorical question is that it is the Lord who has done these great things. The Book of Job is said to be the earliest book of the Bible written. In it Job is recorded saying, "He stretches out the north over the void and hangs the earth on nothing" (26:7).

Congratulations to these scientists on their exciting discovery. Once again we are left breathless at the wonder of this enormous, complex, and beautiful universe. But, once again, man only discovers what the Lord God created; let the true praise go to him.

> *Praise to the Lord, the Almighty, the King of Creation*
> *O my soul, praise Him, for He is thy health and salvation!*
> *All ye who hear,*
> *Now to His temple draw near,*
> *Join me in glad adoration!*[20]

---

[20] "Praise to the Lord the Almighty." Words: Joachim Neander; translated by Catherine Winkworth.

IN THE PRESENCE OF THE GREAT DIGNITARY

Why do we feel compelled to start speaking as soon as we bow our heads to pray? Somewhere along the way we started to pray the same way everyone else does. When we are alone it would feel strange to sit in silence and not say anything, especially *in front of God.* In group prayer silence is scary. It unnerves us. We think *Oh no, something is wrong. Nobody's praying!* They are, just not out loud.

I think there is a proper place for a few seconds of silent pause before we pray. Let me explain.

Would you ever enter a room where your spouse or loved one was and, without acknowledging them as a person, start rattling off a shopping list of requests? Of course, not, right? What about if you were invited into the presence of a great dignitary, a head of state? You would likely give that person the customary honor they are due. That is called reverence. It is acknowledging that this person holds a position of significance. Their level of status, of importance, is greater than mine, and I acknowledge with my reverence before them.

If we would hold ourselves in quiet reverence for a moment before earthly dignitaries, why not before the Great Dignitary, the Lord Almighty? When it comes to God, I am puzzled by how we feel it is perfectly acceptable to barge into his presence and talk without a second's reverence for who we are addressing. He is the Lord; we are not. Yes, to the Christian he is "Our Father," so there is familiarity and privilege. I am not advocating dead formality in our prayers.

Pleasant Places

Nor am I advocating the call to Silence mystics try to beguile us. I assure you, their outward religiosity only testifies that they do not know the free grace of God. I am saying, though, that he is "in Heaven" and we are not. He is the Sovereign One, the one to whom all creation in Heaven, on earth, and under the earth is subject. It only takes a fraction of a second to compose, setting aside our busy thoughts to check ourselves before him. Doing so, I believe, shows him the highest honor and reverence as we approach his eternal throne. It shows we are thinking, aware that we are addressing our Father, our Savior, our Comforter, yet also the One who is the Triune God of the universe to whom honor is due.

There is my challenge: Start your prayers with silence. Take a moment—a second or two—to collect yourself. Acknowledge his lordship, majesty, and splendor through reverence. The more we honor the Lord, the more we will enjoy *him* above all else. Or, as John Piper says, "God is most glorified in us when we are most satisfied in Him."

PETER'S EVANGELISM NOTES, PART I

Luke records this story for us in Acts 10:34-38:

> So Peter opened his mouth and said: "Truly I understand that God shows no partiality, but in every nation anyone who fears him and does what is right is acceptable to him. As for the word that he sent to Israel, preaching good news of peace through Jesus Christ (he is Lord of all), you yourselves know what happened throughout all Judea, beginning from Galilee after the baptism that John proclaimed: how God anointed Jesus of Nazareth with the Holy Spirit and with power. He went about doing good and healing all who were oppressed by the devil, for God was with him.

Only after his blanket "Kill and eat" object lesson did Peter fully grasp the truth that the door of salvation was swung wide open for *everyone* (v34-35). In verse 38, Peter says, "how God anointed Jesus of Nazareth with the Holy Spirit and with power. He went about doing good and healing all who were oppressed by the devil, for God was with him." In very few words, Peter describes the earthly ministry of the Lord to his hearers. If we look at the verses above, in verses 36-37, Peter says that the people in that region knew about Jesus. They had heard of his life, his good deeds, his healings. Why did Peter tell them again? He did not assume it was OK to skip over the facts of the Lord's ministry. He (and others) continued to describe Jesus' ministry to the lost, even if they were already familiar with the stories. There is a lesson in this for us.

Pleasant Places

In America, we Christians tend to skip what Jesus did while he was on the earth when we witness. I think we make two mistakes, albeit well-meaning ones. First we assume everyone already knows. Second, we want to get to sin and the cross, and the need to repent and believe. Like explaining a movie at the climax of the plot, we tend to evangelize from the cross, forward. I know I have been guilty of this. As the world moves further away from Christianity, people have less knowledge of who Jesus is or what he did. Peter considers his audience, though taking nothing for granted. In doing that, he offers us a great example to follow.

Peter's Evangelism Notes, Part II

In Part I we saw in Luke's account about how Peter included statements telling people what Jesus did during his earthly ministry, and *then* pointed them to the cross. Let's continue by looking at Acts 10:39-43 and notice a few other things:

> And we are witnesses of all that he did both in the country of the Jews and in Jerusalem. They put him to death by hanging him on a tree, but God raised him on the third day and made him to appear, not to all the people but to us who had been chosen by God as witnesses, who ate and drank with him after he rose from the dead. And he commanded us to preach to the people and to testify that he is the one appointed by God to be judge of the living and the dead. To him all the prophets bear witness that everyone who believes in him receives forgiveness of sins through his name."

In verses 39-41, Peter continues his summary of the life and ministry of Jesus. As we discussed previously, we Christians (again, at least in America it seems) often overlook sharing about Jesus' life with those who are lost, tending to focus exclusively on the cross and his resurrection.

Look at verse 42, Peter provides a whole picture of Jesus' life, death, and resurrection and then logically shows that Jesus has taken his rightful place as the ultimate Judge each of us will stand before. In verse 43 Peter is quick to include the prophets' own testimony of the coming Christ, something we neglect to at least mention in passing—that

Pleasant Places

Jesus' coming was promised long ago. Then Peter, in a crescendo of testimony, explains how his hearers can be saved by this One he has described.

In a very short span of time, Peter covers a lot of important ground with his hearers:

- Long ago God promised to send a Savior to save people from their sins
- Jesus was that promised Messiah
- Jesus' earthly good deeds, healings, grace, truth, kindness, message, etc. all bear witness of that fact
- His death on the cross was substitutionary, for the sins of his people
- He rose from the dead on the third day
- His now seated as our Judge (hence, a judgment is coming)
- All the prophets (that is to say, all of Scripture), center on Jesus
- Forgiveness of sins is through believing in him

It may not be possible to cover all of this ground at one time. Peter did here but, as my pastor mentioned in his sermon today, Paul sometimes had to reason over months, or even years (Acts 19:8-10). Even if a person does not respond with repentance and faith in that moment, God may be using you to clear up misconceptions they picked up in the past. You may be the one to break up the fallow ground so another can come along and plant the seed, and another will come after that person and water it. As we share the message of the Gospel let's be sure to present it accurately and patiently, and trust God for the results.

Prepare the Way, Everyday

"Prepare the way of the LORD, Make his paths straight" (Mark 1:3, quoting Isaiah 40:3).

One way to apply this verse to our lives is to realize that every day we, as Christians—professed followers of Jesus Christ above and apart from all others—have a duty to prepare the way of the Lord *in our hearts*. We can do this by acknowledging our sins, our laziness, and frankly, our unwillingness to follow which occurs a hundred times a day in our hearts. We make his paths straight when we acknowledge these things and seek the Lord's forgiveness. Then by faith we begin anew with him, trusting in his mercy.

When we prepare the way of the Lord and make his paths straight in our hearts each day, we get rid of the clutter so our King would have unimpeded access in our lives, which is what he both deserves and demands.

Principles of Prayer

When I lived in Tampa, Florida I had the privilege of facilitating a monthly mens prayer breakfast at church. It was great. It was usually only eight or ten men, mostly retirees, the pastor, and me. If you are a young man and never volunteered to hang out with the older guys at church, don't pass up every opportunity you get; they are priceless. As I write I think of faces and I can't help but smile. I think of guys like Len, Aubrey, Denzil, Mac, Ernie, Ron, Clyde, Jeff, Steve, and Pastor Pete. They didn't know it, but to me those guys transformed an hour over coffee and donuts into a glimpse of heaven.

I gave what follows as a devotional to the men one Saturday. The principles below are not all-inclusive; nor are they magical, mystical formulas. Our first motive to pray should be the desire to spend time with Lord. Hopefully these ideas help make those times more fruitful.

- Make time
- Get alone
- Prepare your heart
- Pour out your heart
- Thank and praise him

Make Time

Read Mark 1:32-36. After an already long day of ministry (see previous verses of chapter), evening comes. Jesus' work day, however, is not over. He has hours of ministry that evening with the townspeople who lined up outside the place where he stayed. You and I might be quick to excuse sleeping-in the next morning—it was a late night, afterall. Not Jesus. He gets up "very early" and goes off to be with his Father (see 1:32a, 34b, and 35). Lesson: Attack the calendar if you must. Ask God to wake you up early. Get up in the middle of the night. Whatever it takes, be alone with the Lord. As Pastor Pete taught us once, *We make time for the things we want to do.*

GET ALONE

The whole town was where he was; he needed to get alone. Jesus sought solitude. The disciples had to go out looking for him. For us, getting alone often means no family, phone, email, responsibilities, commitments, noise or other distractions. I get distracted by the tick-tock of a clock on the wall after a few minutes. It used to really drive me crazy. I do better with it now. Still, if that kind of thing is a distraction, remove it. This does not mean we have to pray in silence. It means we remove whatever hinders our time with God from being the most it can be. Like Jesus said in Matthew 6:6, go to your room, close the door and pray in secret. Jesus not only instructs us to seek out alone time with the Lord, he models it.

PREPARE YOUR HEART

There are three groups to think about with this principle. First, make sure your heart is clean and prepared with the Lord. Mark 1:3b - "Prepare the way of the Lord." A Presidential advance team goes weeks ahead of the President's scheduled trip to set everything in order for his arrival. In ancient times a similar routine was done for ancient kings to ensure obstacle-free travel along the roads. This verse primarily refers to the coming of Jesus in his earthly ministry, but in a sense it applies to us as well, reminding us to prepare our heart daily to fellowship with our Creator. In other words: Get rid of obstacles--deal with sin; get serious. Be thoughtful and reverent. Second, men, prepare your heart with your wife (1 Peter 3:7). Imagine going to spend time with your earthly father-in-law if you are mistreating or angry with his daughter.[21] Third, prepare your heart with everyone else. In Matthew 5:23, 24 Jesus teaches us to be reconciled with our brother (or sister) if an offense comes to mind.

Pour Out Your Heart

Psalm 62:5-8 (emphasis on v8). What does God not already know? You won't surprise him in your confession. Don't be like Adam and Eve, wrapping yourself in fig leaves and excuses. Get it all out on the table of prayer. The Holy Spirit will help you. Intercession for others also happens here as he reminds you of others to pray for. Pauses and breaks are OK as you grow your "prayer muscles." So is catching yourself when your mind wanders—mine does often. The Lord is gracious and patient. Pray intelligently, respectfully, reverently. Pray as to a King, yet to a friend. You don't have to pray in "King James" English, the point is simply to be honest and have respect.

Thank and Praise Him

He is worthy. He hears your prayer. He will answer. He loves his children. He gives the Spirit to lead us. The Holy Spirit is our Comforter and Helper. The reasons to give thanks and praise to the Lord are as infinite as he is.

---

[21] I heard this from Baptist missionary and preacher Paul Washer in a sermon or lecture, but I can't exactly recall which, so I am acknowledging him generally.

Putting It All Into Practice

We will never master prayer. That is not the point. The point is communion with God, spending time with him. What matters is praying. In prayer God changes us. Prayer humbles us before our Father and quiets us down from our anxious thoughts that we would remember to wait on him in faith. Christians are not called to be a perfect people in this world; but our Lord does call us to be a praying people.

Pleasant Places

WORSHIP THROUGH EVANGELISM

Are you trying in some way every day to reconcile sinners with God? Jesus has given us the Great Commission (Matthew 28:19-20) to go and make disciples. And he has given us the ministry of reconciliation (2 Corinthians 5:18). Paul told the Colossian church, "him we preach, warning every man" (1:28). When was the last time you warned anyone with a word, a tract, a letter...*something*?

In Exodus 3:12 the Lord says to Moses, "But I will be with you, and this shall be the sign for you, that I have sent you: when you have brought the people out of Egypt, you shall serve God on this mountain." John MacArthur notes, "Israel would not be delivered simply out of bondage and oppression, but *rescued to worship*" (emphasis added). [22] I love that. This story and that phrase apply to our lives as well. God sent his only Son to rescue us from sin and death. We, too, are "rescued to worship." One way in which we do that is to be sure to tell others how they too can be rescued.

---

[22] John MacArthur, The MacArthur Bible Commentary. 2005, Thomas Nelson, Nashville

Anthony F. Russo

"There is but a Step Between Me and Death"

The title of this essay comes from David's words in 1 Samuel 20:3. That is how he describes to Jonathan where he finds himself. Jonathan's father, Saul, the king of Israel, has forsaken the Lord. As a consequence and judgment against him, the Lord sent a "distressing spirit" to vex him. Saul's warped perception of reality sees his most loyal subject, David, as his most dangerous threat. As Saul seeks to kill him, David is literally on the run trying to save his own life.

The first thing to consider is that there came a point when, for his own safety, David had to leave the presence of Saul. As Christians we are called to often take what is the hard road and endure trials and suffering. I have read missionary stories of times of persecution when missionaries decided to stay and also times when they felt it best to flee. David's life was in real danger. David himself thought his life was in danger. David knew it was time to go.

But the larger truth was that David was in no danger at all. God was with him. David was hand-picked by God to replace Saul as king. The prophet Samuel obeyed the Lord's command and anointed David with oil as the sign of his imminent reign over Israel. David was only a youth tending his father's flocks at that time. The Lord confirmed this call by soon after moving David into service first as King Saul's personal musician, then his chief general. Then, through repeated military victories, the Lord gave David increasing favor among his countrymen, "all Israel and Judah loved David" (1 Sam 18:15). God would accomplish through David

Pleasant Places

exactly what he planned regardless of rebellious, desperate Saul or anyone else

God allowed what he did in David's life, using people and events as his tools of pressure and heat to forge David into a man useful for greater service to himself—and he may be doing the same to you. You may, with David, lower your head and cry, "There is but a step between me and death." Learn from God's man. Trust in the Lord.

WAITING

> David departed from there and escaped to the cave of Adullam. And when his brothers and all his father's house heard it, they went down there to him. And everyone who was in distress, and everyone who was in debt, and everyone who was bitter in soul, gathered to him. And he became commander over them. And there were with him about four hundred men.
>
> And David went from there to Mizpeh of Moab. And he said to the king of Moab, "Please let my father and my mother stay with you, till I know what God will do for me." And he left them with the king of Moab, and they stayed with him all the time that David was in the stronghold (1 Samuel 22:1-4).

THE KING IN WAITING BECOMES THE KING IN HIDING

I have only been in a few caves in my life. The first cave I remember was Crystal Cave in Pennsylvania. I have also been to Ruby Falls in Chattanooga, Tennessee and Mammoth Cave outside of Louisville, Kentucky. All of them are commercial caves. Tourist attractions, complete with lighting, handrails, and of course, a gift shop. David did not visit the cave of Adullam as tourist. This verse says he escaped there.

The anointed-king-in-waiting was, at present, the anointed-king-in-hiding. He was being hunted by Saul, from whom the Lord's favor had departed. He had also recently dodged another king—Achish of Gath—who was king over one of five chief cities of Israel's arch-enemy of the day, the Philistines.

Adullam was about 17 miles southwest of Jerusalem and 10 miles southeast of Gath. It is here, geographically and chronologically in the story where we meet up with David in 1 Samuel 22:1. This time of waiting in David's life offers many lessons to us. It is a short passage but, like all Scripture, is profitable for our training (2 Timothy 3:16).

For a fuller treatment of this passage, I highly recommend Alan Redpath's *The Making of a Man of God: Studies in the Life of David*.[23] I won't do it justice in one brief sentence, but Redpath shows that just as "everyone who was in distress…in debt…and discontented gathered to [David]…" David was a picture of Christ. Like those running to David for safety and shepherding, we who are distressed by our sin, indebted by our sin, and discontented in our sin can find protection and peace through the great Son of David, Jesus.

How Long?

David honors his parents by bringing them to the Moabite king so he would protect them while his own life, by all natural appearances, was in grave danger. This detail includes something important: a period of time. Exactly how long we don't know, though the text says, "and they dwelt with him all the time David was in the stronghold."

In a spiritual sense, we know *exactly* how long it was. It was exactly as long as the Lord determined it to be, and not one

---

[23] Alan Redpath. *The Making of a Man of God: Studies in the Life of David.* Revell Books.

second longer. The Lord is sovereign; he can do what he pleases. God loves us, but he never abdicated his sovereignty over all things. It was the Lord who chose David to eventually be king and would one day raise him up for such a purpose. But, for now, it was the Lord who allowed this time of waiting in David's life.

Why did the Lord work things this way? That is between the Lord and David. But we can surmise at least a couple reasons: One reason is it gave time for people to come and find their safe harbor in David. Another is that God was honing David's leadership skills. Of course, God was also working in David's life to make him ever more reliant upon him.

Believer, how long is your time in your Adullum? I don't know and neither do you. However long God has you hidden away in there, use the time to take stock of the goodness of God, and "forget not his mercies and love." That line comes from Psalm 34, which David wrote shortly before his time at Adullum.

Just as he did with David, God will use your times in your own Adullum to discipline you, to grow you, and to accomplish whatever purposes he has for you and others around you. Keep trusting the Lord. David's time in the cave didn't last forever, and neither will yours.

Songs in the Night

If Psalm 34 was written by David shortly before the events that led to his hiding in the cave, do we have any writings of his from when he was actually in the cave? Thankfully, in God's good providence the answer is yes, we have two:

Pleasant Places

Psalm 142 and Psalm 57. Psalm 142, although it appears later in the Psalms, seems to have been written first. For one thing, it seems darker and more desperately clinging to God. Also, (and I didn't catch this myself and don't remember who to attribute it to) David writes that "there is no one who acknowledges me...no one cares for my soul" (verse 4).

Psalm 57 is, by contrast, lighter than Psalm 142. Yes, his soul "is amidst the lions" and cruel men are after him (verses 4 and 6). But David writes that he will hide in the shadow of the wings of the Lord, making God his shelter until this storm passes (verse 1). And unlike the desperate cries of 142, David seems to have come to a place of understanding and trust that God has not forsaken him. There are still questions. He is still living out of a cave and his life is still in danger (humanly speaking), but his heart is calmer and settled: "My heart is steadfast, O God, my heart is steadfast; I will sing and make melody" (verse 7).

David escaped to a cave and poured his heart out to God and God gave him peace amidst the strife. David didn't say the cave was his refuge. Rather, he said the Lord was his refuge (Psalm 142:5 and Psalm 57:1). Jesus tells us to go to our rooms, close the door, and pray in secret—to get alone with the Lord. Like David, until we make God our refuge our hearts cannot get settled and steadfast.

OUR ADULLUM

So what should our attitude be while we wait on the Lord?

I passed over it without comment earlier, but I want to bring to your attention the qualifier David includes in his request to the King of Moab regarding how long his (David's) parents should live with the king: " ...til I know what God will do for me." David didn't say "...til I figure out how to get myself out of this mess." In this trying circumstance David was determined to let God direct the next steps. As he did he used the situation to testify to the king about God and his faithfulness. As hard as it is for us, if we name Christ as Lord, we absolutely, resolutely wait on him for our orders. And while we wait, let us follow David's example of using the time to testify to others of God's faithfulness in all things.

David, as I mentioned, was determined to stay in the stronghold of the cave until the Lord directed him otherwise. He knew that to leave early and go his own way was sin. We know, as I pointed out earlier, by the multiplicity of events in this passage that they could not have all happened on a single day. Verse 4 records how David's parents stayed with the king, "all the time that David was in the stronghold." David was waiting for some time. How long that was we don't exactly know, although it was long enough for several key events to happen.

First, it was long enough for his family to find out and travel to visit him (v1). Second, it was long enough for others to find out and eventually come to have him as their captain (v2). Third, it was long enough for him to travel to Mizpah and back (v3).

WHEN THE WAITING IS OVER

As Peter tells us many, many years later, "the Lord is not slow to fulfill his promise" (2 Peter 3:9). Look what happens next in the story: "Now the prophet Gad said to David, 'Do not remain in the stronghold; depart, and go into the land of Judah'" (v5).

God answered.

It was time to leave the cave.

God spoke. He sent David's eviction notice through his servant, Gad. It was time to move out.

Just moments before he got the news it would've been sin for David to leave the cave and journey somewhere else. Now God has spoken and it would be sin to stay. This is how God often leads his children. Remember when, in effect, God kept telling Noah, "Not yet" but then he gave the go-ahead? Think of all the times over their forty years in the desert God had Israel stay camped where they were? It was sometimes a short time, sometimes a long time. But then the cloudy pillar would move and it was time to go. If you haven't already, you too will have times where God says "Wait" and then times when he says "Go."

So what did David do? Verse 5 tells us, "So David departed and went into the forest of Hereth." David waited on the Lord, listened to the counsel of the godly, and obeyed God. Waiting on God is as simple as that. The working out of that is certainly easier said than done, but there is greater stress and frustration in store when we do not follow God's leading than when we do.

PUTTING IT ALL TOGETHER
Some final thoughts then.

Remember what David wrote in Psalm 34, namely, keep trusting God.

Be faithful in the things God has called you while you wait, including being faithful in your roles as a husband/wife, father/mother, church member, worker, etc.

Expectancy–Wait for God to lead you. Remember the words David wrote during this time (particularly Psalms 57:1-3 and 142:7). David left his life in the Lord's hands entirely.

Remember all the examples in the bible of men and women who were taught to wait and God did not forget any of them. He never abandoned one of them in their trials. In due time–in his time–he brought each one safely to where he was leading them. And the same is true for you and for me. God is faithful.

DO NOT BE DECEIVED

> Now as he sat on the Mount of Olives, the disciples came to Him privately, saying, "Tell us, when will these things be? And what will be the sign of Your coming, and of the end of the age?"
>
> And Jesus answered and said to them: "Take heed that no one deceives you" (Matthew 24:3-4 NKJV).

A few years ago I was rereading this passage and, as often happens with Scripture, I noticed something I had not seen before. If you were Jesus and the disciples asked you when the terrible things you just described would happen, would your first answer be, 'don't be deceived'?

To understand how strange this sounds at first hearing, imagine the question was about something more ordinary:

What time is dinner?

"Don't be fooled."

Do you feel the peculiar weight of his words now? If it wasn't from Jesus himself it would be an odd reply, wouldn't it? Yet it is the brilliance of God. Jesus is telling them—and us—that the primary thing we need to know about the time when God is close to bringing an end to this age is that there will be a great risk of deception. We had better be on guard.

Sadly, I can think of many examples of famous preachers being touted (or touting themselves) as great teachers, but they teach things that do not align with the word of God. The same is true with secular self-help gurus, advice columnists, and talk show hosts. They are regarded as people of influence, but what terrible influences they are!

Jesus says you and I must discern for ourselves truth from error. We are to evaluate everything we read and hear and see and compare it against what the Bible says.[24] To be a Christian is to be a thinker.

Never, ever forget Jesus' words. We are in the last days and there are many false teachers. How do I know? Because the one who does not lie told us so.

---

[24] This includes what you read of my words, too!

A Dynasty of Grace

Seminary students are privileged to hear many guest speakers. In my first semester of seminary we had the best guest speaker when Rev. Bill Iverson, and his grown son Daniel (the third), spoke at our school.

Bill, as he preferred to be called, had been a church planter for over 60 years. At 82 years old, he was considered by some to be the greatest living evangelist of the PCA denomination.[25] I did not know this when I met him, and he was far too unassuming to acknowledge the accolade anyway.

The lineage of Iversons in ministry is a long and godly one. It was Bill's grandfather, Halvor, who first became a Christian back in Norway. His son, Daniel, grew to become a minister and wrote the famous chorus, "Spirit of the Living God, Fall Afresh on Me." More than that, Daniel Iverson also planted 21 churches and over the course of his ministry sent over 150 ministers and missionaries out. His son, Daniel II, was a WWII military hero who later was killed in a military training exercise. For many years a missionary plane in the Congo bore his name in tribute. Bill's son, also Daniel (Daniel III, the one who also spoke that day), has been serving in Japan as a missionary pastor for almost a quarter of a century. Daniel IV and I started at seminary at the same time and shared classes together. Already a veteran of inner-city ministry, he is carrying on the Iverson dynasty of grace now at a church in Atlanta, Georgia.

---

[25] PCA = Presbyterian Church in America.

Anthony F. Russo

To be honest, there is so much Christian heritage and so many stories in the Iverson family tree that it makes it hard to keep them all straight. Do a web search and you'll see what I mean. There are at least six Christ-following generations of Iversons on earth or now in Heaven, and thousands of souls have been rescued through this one family's combined evangelistic labors. Halvor and Ervine Iverson were simply a husband and wife in Norway in the 1800s who loved Jesus. And now look at "what God hath wrought" all these many years later.

I am not a parent, but one lesson here is for parents. Think how you raise your children does not have much impact on their lives? Think again. Pray regularly with them and for them. Fill their growing hearts and minds with the Scriptures. Model Christ to them. Let them see you love others. And trust the Lord to do far beyond what you could ever dream. You don't know what the Lord's plans are. You might be the first generation in a dynasty of grace.

Pleasant Places

TROUBLE PRAYING?

Prayer and those pharmaceutical commercials on TV rarely have anything in common. (Although, generally speaking, if more people did the former, they might not need the latter…) However, let me ask you some diagnostic questions like those commercials do:

Are you tired?

Restless?

Finding it hard to concentrate?

I do not know about you, but those complaints are often my own complaints about my prayer life. I can be wide awake when I go to pray and instantly get sleepy…or fidgety…or I start a sentence in prayer and two seconds later I am a million mental miles away. So, yes, I have trouble praying. How about you?

Sometime ago I picked up a used reprint of Andrew Murray's, *The Prayer Life*. I have read lots of books on prayer. Most seem to tell me over and over of the importance of prayer, the necessity of prayer, and what an utter abject failure of a Christian I am that I even need to read a book on prayer. (Well, that is how I feel by the time I finish them.) None of my practical questions are answered. I am so thankful Murray's book is different.

Murray was a Dutch Reformed minister whose often spoke and wrote on prayer. As Murray himself says in the foreword, the book came about as a result of lectures he gave at a conference of ministers in South Africa in 1912. The conference took a Divinely-appointed detour as one-by-one those gathered confessed their own prayerlessness before God. Murray was asked to compile his lectures on the subject into written form for distribution afterwards.

Chapter 9, "Hints for the Inner Chamber", is my favorite chapter because of its practical helps. Next time you get alone with the Lord (which I hope is everyday) enjoy yourself and step through these helpful hints:

- Get alone, then start with thanks to God for everything and talk to him freely
- Bible study, and praying with your Bible, is essential
- After a time praying over a few verses and thinking on them, pray
- Pray for your needs, then also take full advantage of the privilege to pray for others
- Prayer does not end at "amen." A life of consistent Christian living is just as important

Growing into a praying person takes time, like any other skill. I am so glad the Lord helps us and promises to bless our investments of time and devotion as we seek to be more prayerful children.

Pleasant Places

I KNOW A SECRET

Imagine going to an event where everyone is wearing those familiar blue and white "Hello My Name is…" stickers. Imagine you meet someone and theirs says, *Hello, My Name is SECRET*. That'd be unusual, wouldn't it? Well, that is exactly what I thought when I saw a young woman wearing it one night.

I was driving home one night and stopped into a pharmacy. The young girl at the cash register was wearing her name tag, but her name was "Secret." I was instantly surprised and curious. Was it a slow night in the store, prompting her and her coworkers to make up silly name badges? Was she unwilling to tell people her name? There was a story there and I wanted to know it. I am glad I took the time to notice and ask, because I've never forgotten it. Even now, years later, it comes to mind.

Thankfully it *was* a slow night in the store so I could ask her about it. It wasn't a prank; her name really was Secret. When I asked her if she would mind telling me the story she was kind to oblige. Her parents were told they could not have children. They prayed and the Lord heard their prayers. She was the baby who was the answer to their prayers. Her father named her Secret after the song that goes, "It is no secret what God can do."

I told her she had a beautiful name and thanked her for sharing her story with me. What a blessing. Her parents sought to honor the Lord, grateful for what he had done. No matter where in life her decisions would take her, her name would be a testimony to their love for him and a reminder to her that she was the answer to their prayers all those years ago. Every time her name is mentioned or appears in print—on a form, a license, or a corner pharmacy name badge—it is a declaration of praise and thanksgiving to the Lord for the little one he blessed her parents with.

That is a Secret worth sharing.

Pleasant Places

WHAT HAVE YOU DONE WITH THE BIBLE?

> And we also thank God constantly for this, that when you received the word of God, which you heard from us, you accepted it not as the word of men but as what it really is, the word of God, which is at work in you believers" (1 Thessalonians 2:13).

> There is dust enough on some of your Bibles to write 'damnation' with your fingers.
> - Charles Spurgeon

I am a thrift store guy. Always have been. I grew up in a lower-middle class family so I was raised on closeout stores, thrift stores, garage sales and flea markets. I'm always excited to find a new one to look around see what's there.

One thing I noticed there on a shelf was a beautiful wooden box, about 8x6" or so. It was a carefully varnished keepsake box with a cross on the top. Inside was a Bible. I watched a lady pick it up, open the box, leaf through the pages of the Bible, and then close it and move on other *stuff*. I wondered if she know anything about the book inside? Did she ever read it? Did the person who donated it ever read it? Did they keep it around as some sort of religious good-luck charm? I had no intention of buying it but I was curious about the response it would trigger in the hundreds of people who would stop to look at it until someone buys it.

This morning in my Bible reading I read Paul's commendation the believers at Thessalonica for how they received the word of God. He says they didn't receive it merely as the words of men but as it was: the word of God himself.

Just like the lady looking at that keepsake Bible, most people in America have already encountered the Bible in their life. What has been your reaction to it? What have you done with the Bible? Have you dismissed it as religious lore? Maybe just the opposite. Maybe you regard it as some religious relic no home should be without. Some people protect it in an out of sight place like a decorative box or on some shelf full of other books they really have no intention of ever reading. Some people arch their back self-righteously and protest the need to read it. *Oh I believe the Bible—but I don't read it.* If any of this describes you then, to use the Apostle Paul's words, you are receiving God's words as though they were merely the words of men.

There are only two choices in how you or I handle the Bible (and I don't mean the physical book of ink and paper), either we dismiss it as the words of men or receive it as the word of God.

Pleasant Places

A WALK THROUGH A CEMETERY

I heard the story at seminary how a preaching professor took his students to a cemetery. They were to stand there in the field of headstones and preach to the people in the graves, to try to call them to life. His point was powerful: The Bible says men and women are "dead" in their sin. The preacher has no more ability to preach someone into being a Christian than the hearer does of responding. Dead people don't respond. Salvation is a supernatural work of God. God must raise the hearer from the death of their sin if they are to be saved. Still, God also calls the man of God to be faithful in preaching to dead sinners every chance he gets.

With this story in mind, one day I went to a cemetery near my house. I wanted to walk around and imagine myself as a student in that class to let the full weight of the object lesson sink in.

Jesus said that the broad road leads to destruction and many go that way, but the road that leads to life is narrow and only a few find it (Matthew 7:13-14). As I looked across the landscape of grass and granite I wondered how many of the people trusted Christ for salvation. By Jesus' own words, I was sad to think the majority did not.

And then, yes, I stood there in the cemetery and preached the Gospel among the graves.

But I also walked around, looking at the headstones and thinking about the people underneath me. I was surrounded by people who didn't talk, but they sure said a lot.

For one thing, they told me I really do need to make my final arrangements in case I should die unexpectedly. Actually, looking out across the field their names and dates etched in stone corrected me: No one dies unexpectedly. We all expect to die some day; for some it is just sooner than they expect.

When you sit and look at someone's final resting place it is a common grace of God that it makes you think about your own mortality. It is a divine pause to jar unbelievers into questioning what happens after death. For the believer it gives supernatural clarity that Christianity, indeed, is the one true faith that provides all the answers and sufficiently, properly prepares a person for eternity.

I spent about 20 minutes sitting on a memorial bench facing James Crawford's grave. You ask, *Who is James Crawford?* I don't know. His grave had a bench and offered shade, so I sat down and pondered the life of the man interred before me.

Here is what I did and didn't learn about James W. Crawford: I know his name, but not all of it. I know his birth day and year, and I know when he died. I know where he is buried, but I don't know where he was born or lived or died.

Based on the name he shared his headstone with, I know he was married. I know what his wife's name was, and the dates she was born and died. I do not know when they married or how long they were married. Nor do I know if they were happily married (I hope so). Was she his only wife? Second wife? Tenth wife? Did they have children? If so, how many? If not, why not? So many questions.

Pleasant Places

What about James the man? What did he do for a living? What adventures or sorrows did he experience? What was his favorite color? Did he have hobbies? Was his laugh loud and contagious, or a kind of quiet, dry chuckle? Or maybe his life was a crush of sorrows or fury or bitterness and he never laughed at all. I don't know.

I can't answer many questions about James W. Crawford because all that his left of him in this world is a gray marble slab etched with cold, lifeless facts.

For most of us this life is short, unpredictable, and ultimately encapsulated in about 50 characters on a rock in a field.

After my time with Mr. Crawford I kept walking. As the sole representative of the land of the living, I walked around reading names and dates, doing mental calculations of their lives as I went. People don't really call them "tombstones" anymore, do they? That sounds too much like death, I guess. They used to be called grave markers, but that too seems to have fallen out of vogue. "Headstones" is the preferred word to use nowadays, I think. The sanitized word, perhaps. We may fool ourselves about death while we're alive, but I can assure you no one around me was fooled.

Epitaphs were popular many years ago. I remember hearing an Irish tombstone limerick one time. I can't remember it now, but it had that wry, earthy humor the Irish are famous for. Graves of the American Old West were often colorful quips about the departed too. I don't know if familial creativity has diminished or the prices for memorials now are charged by the character, but I didn't see many epitaphs inscribed, witty or otherwise. An epitaph may be a person's only lasting declaration on this earth. Words meant to embody your entire life etched into marble as a lasting monument of *you*.

What would be your epitaph? Would your epitaph reflect your life on the broad road or the narrow one? If you are unsure, I would plead with you to make certain you are safely trusting in Christ alone for salvation. Then you can rejoice that your legacy in this world will read like these I found:

> "SAVED BY GRACE"
> ಶ
> LARRY B. GLOVER, II
> Born: January 13, 1972
> Born Again: December, 1978
> Past Away: April 26, 1988
> ಶ
> "I TRUSTED IN GOD"

A Final Word: We're Almost Home

Christian, when was the last time you let your mind wander and wonder about *Home*? Stop and savor the longing you have in your heart for the rest that awaits you in heaven. Does your head hang down in this sin-heavy world? Have the eyes of your heart forgotten how to look upward? If today was "just another Monday" for you, spend a few moments enveloped in the joy of Heaven, your true home.

For now things are imperfect. Yes, every day in this life we grieve our Lord with our sins. Yes, doubts so easily cloud our hearts and obscure the Son. Yes, we are brought low through circumstances, sickness, and even the Lord's discipline sometimes. Even so, our feeble, fledgling attempts to honor the Lord each day down here please him up there. He rewards the simplest act of Christian grace—even giving a cup of water in Jesus' name—with incalculable interest from his bottomless treasures. And the best reward is himself.

So, while it is day there remains work to do. Be faithful in what God has given you to do, and I will—with his help—do the same. Let's recommit ourselves to prayer, to the Scriptures, to obedience, to evangelism, and to serving the Church as she seeks to make God's name great among the nations (Malachi 1:11).

Thank you for reading this book. Thank you for the time you have kindly given me. I hope you are encouraged. I hope you finish this book having gained some benefit. I hope that you received something and can pass it on to someone else.

My final words to you today, Christian, are words of hope. Do not grow weary; do not faint. Though the joy of your Heavenly home seems a long way off, do not get caught up in the grind of this world to lose sight of the beauty that *will* be yours someday soon. Ask any elderly saint and they'll tell you that in no time at all your life will fly by fast. And soon you and I will be with the Savior in the most Pleasant Place of all.